I0434721

Black Thoughts
for
White America

Black Thoughts
for
White America

G. Woody Lamonte

Writers Club Press
New York Lincoln Shanghai

Black Thoughts for White America

All Rights Reserved © 2002 by G. Woody Lamonte

No part of this book may be reproduced or transmitted in any form or by any means, graphic, electronic, or mechanical, including photocopying, recording, taping, or by any information storage retrieval system, without the written permission of the publisher.

Writers Club Press
an imprint of iUniverse, Inc.

For information address:
iUniverse, Inc.
2021 Pine Lake Road, Suite 100
Lincoln, NE 68512
www.iuniverse.com

ISBN: 0-595-26165-5

Printed in the United States of America

To Rev., Sister Daisy & Sonny

Contents

(Courtesy of the Web)

Forewarned

A sizeable portion of white America knows next to nothing about black people, including those in this country and on the rest of the planet as well. It has been said white America believes that black history started with Jackie Robinson. In a sense this statement is valid since with his appearance, it was the first time many of them actually bothered to turn their attention and interest toward a black person. Up until that time and even for a great number of white folk today, black people and people of color in general, were and are just part of the scenery–not really human, but a facsimile that's been provided to do their bidding.

In our time, many in this young nation have discovered that our collective planetary history includes civilizations and systems created by black and brown humans (non-whites) that have long since left the scene. The evidence of their presence is still with us today and can no longer be ignored.

The study of things Kemetian (Egyptian), a black civilization, has always fascinated my white brother. However, his interest in that culture is primarily confined to the last 300 or so years of the 4000+year existence of that system. People like himself governed this latter part. In today's world, representations of things Egyptian take on a decided European caste. Only real and dedicated scholars have bothered to study the part of that culture when native Africans were the leaders.

On this side of the planet, we have recently deciphered the writings of the Mayans, Incas and Aztecs, civilizations designed and constructed by brown people. They were coming to their cyclical end when the white man showed up on their doorstep.

In today's arena where information is dispensed in 30-second visual/ sound clips, not much can be learned about any human endeavor that has never been recognized by white America. Since the outset of this experiment in self-government, my white brother has been and still is primarily talking to and about himself. In today's world with multi-level bombast about diversity, the American colonial perspective still persists when describing other members of our species.

The following is a collection of short essays and poems that allow this writer to express his views on the present evolving system known as the United States of America and the overall activity of our species on this planet. These essays are primarily three pages in length and the poems are all one page each. There are a few exceptions.

HIS-STORY

I heard that one of us wrote a book with the title "Don't Know Much About History". A love song I remember hearing in my timeline talked about not knowing much about geometry or biology either, but he did know that he loved someone.

Like many of us here in this unfolding, I got bored in history class. The way it was presented turned you off to what was going on in those stories. It was dull. Guys would sleep a lot. The girls, knowing that the males weren't interested, got an opportunity to indicate their intellect.

Suppression started early with them—
somewhere at the start of the first millennium—
on this side of the artificial divide.
It's all your fault.

I was on autopilot—living in a self-imposed exile all during high school. In college I took on a full schedule of 18 units my first semester and somewhere within those four years of college, I even did 21 units on one occasion. However, I would not have taken any history voluntarily were it not for the fact that I had to fill up an empty 3-hr slot in my course list. At the end of my sophomore year, my required courses only took up 15 hours, so I picked English History as an elective. Don't ask me why, but I soon found myself sitting in the class of a most fascinating mind. Left an impression on me, this individual did. Both he and his wife were part of the faculty at this "historically black institution", as they are called these days. She was in the Home Economics department, one of the fields wherein women could achieve some recognition, and he was into history.

His idea was that the story, no matter whose it was or is, concerns individuals and the event, not *just* the event. If you concentrate only on the event, it becomes boring. Whereas when you concern yourself with the individual or persons involved in the event, an entirely different perspective is achieved about the event and, indeed, the individual as well.

So, when I use the term his-story, like others before me, it states that history, as it is usually presented to us, is basically the story of one type of human being—male, and not from my tribe. This male carries in his mind ideas and concepts from the history of my tribe but, for some strange reason, he has not ever really bothered much to mention this simple fact. When he does say anything about my tribe and me, it follows a formula, and never really says very much of a positive nature.

In today's world all of us hear from the same individuals, ad naseum. A quick glance at the prevalent visual medium reveals the same people, primarily males, pontificating about planetary events. With the exception of a few predictable areas of the "news", not much is ever said about me and my place on the planet, let alone anything about my history prior to that of my paleface brother.

Consequently, I figure it's up to me to tell my own story, since in reality, it's the only one I'm involved in. I'm certain I've missed many events but hopefully not too many. If I've been successful, then I've been able to learn more and more each marvelous day on how to use all the energies being provided here by our earth mother.

So, here's my take on some his-stories and her-stories of our human family.

The Beginning of Us

If anyone tells you that he or she knows how we came to be here on this living being known now as Earth and offers written evidence to support that belief, then I suggest you put a great distance between you and this particular individual. Spare no expense!!! Get away from this person, quickly.

At this stage of the game we really don't know where we came from, or even if we *are* from here, this planet.

We have many, many different versions of how we came to be—some much, much older than those most citizens of my adolescent homeland believe and accept as gospel.

The basic species creation line that many of our population hold to is the one presented in what Americans call the bible. Since this is just one of the many ancient texts written by our species, a more balanced picture would result when information from other sources is included.

What are these other sources and why haven't we heard of them, you ask.

Many of us have heard of them, if however briefly, but not much is ever said about these other beginning stories in my teenager-of-a-nation. Besides, we all know what happens when you start telling stories we humans have that come from another languages and cultures—SOMETHING GETS LOST IN THE TRANSLATION, even with the forbidden words.

Just one example of those "big translation losses" is that commandment about killing one of our own kind. The original word was murder and NOT kill. These are two different concepts coming out of the gate. The original commandment took into account the fact of self-preservation. Murder has intent and direction, requiring forethought. The act of killing another member of our species happens in so many different new ways in our time, that we've had to readjust our thinking and reaction to its occurrence rather quickly. Just look back over the last one hundred years.

We really didn't know that we would be dealing with death in the automobile and how many of our species we would be killing with these devices, either by design or neglect. We also have the strange capacity to allow the state to kill at will but restrict those instances for the individual. So, there seems to be confusion as to this particular translated commandment and its various interpretations.

From those same beginning stories comes the one describing some of the different kinds of human beings and how they came to be. Mind you, I said some of the human family, because the earliest stories passed along in the bible are incomplete when it comes to describing the entire human family. They seem only to describe just two kinds of humans, black and white, or more precisely, those humans in the particular region of the planet from which these stories arose. We also hear tell of lost tribes. If there were lost tribes, then they were lost in the same region of the planet and not over where we are now.

Also, another interesting point about these particular beginning stories is that those of us considered members of the black tribes are said to be the descendants of one who is committed the first killing on this planet. Over the centuries, the names have become garbled and mixed up, but most Americans adhere strongly to the story of Cain and Abel.

*Come forward in time with this relatively new myth
and one can easily understand the situation
in which we all find ourselves today*

Our species is ancient; we just don't remember all the parts of the story. There is recorded knowledge of this fact but a lot of it was not recorded or transcribed in the fashion westerners are used to. By the time the United States showed up, all the other creation stories of the other human tribes had been discredited for political and/or financial reasons or, in the case of my white brother, simply ignored. In our present time, we have also been distracted by so many unimportant things, many of us don't realize that these other beginning stories are still here with us.

I'm not of those particular tribes, so I must look elsewhere to find my beginnings.

Dude, I Think We're Related

I hail from the 15th state admitted to this work-in-progress called America. When I came to the Golden State, it was the first time I had ever seen or interacted with those members of the human family called Mexican.

You can cook my food, cut my lawn,
clean my home, drive my car,
watch after my kids,
but don't have an opinion.

I recognized that tired game the second I landed at the foot of Broadway in downtown San Diego. So I set about adjusting to the world-at-large's invasion of my world at the behest of the USNavy, affectionately called the Canoe Club. We were gearing up for another one of my paleface brother's insane misuse of our species' intellect and we were calling it Vietnam. The gods smiled on me and I survived that little moneymaking scheme relatively unscathed. However, a lot of us didn't survive and I'm *not* talking about the ones we buried.

So, after the Navy and I parted company, I set about living my own life without their help. I was soon to find out a lot more about these other members of the human family called Mexican.

First off, that's not what most of them are. The word they use to refer to themselves is Mestizos, or those with mixed blood. This word reminds them of their ancestry—those humans my white brother mistakenly calls Indians. Their history and ancestry includes that pyramid-building technology, something I was familiar with when reading about my own tribal history. Imagine my surprise and irritation when I discovered that the largest pyramid ever built on the planet is not in Egypt, as we have been previously told by you-know-who, but actually down there in the Yucatan peninsula. As it her habit, our earth mother has sort of reclaimed the materials used to build this particular structure—she grew the jungle mantel over it. When my white brother, in his Spanish variety, showed up in his discovering phase, they thought it was a mountain and build a church on it.

Typical.

So, I asked myself this question. If these guys had this pyramid-building technology, up to and including observatories that kept track of things stellar, and the guys from my tribe did the same thing, does that not indicate a common source for this knowledge? Mind you, the major portion of my tribe's history had ended long before this present white guy was really awake on our planet.

The members of the original and following white tribes that took over my tribe's country are also gone now or have evolved into modern versions of themselves. Alexander died in his early thirties (ancient rock star—drugs?) and the Romans let their empire get too big and it went broke and there was no one around with enough cash to save it. Nothing drastic here with these events.

Apparently, the guys on this side of the planet had already discovered that little fact about human civilizations and their cyclical collapses and would have told the incoming white boys about it, but they never got a chance to. Gold got in the way.

So along the way I discover these other beginning stories of the Inca, the Maya, the Olmecs, Toltecs, and Aztecs. In addition to these family members, there are many other members of the human family that lived on this side of the planet and who had their own stories to tell. However, for reasons mentioned elsewhere, we've all had our collective attention focused on just one creation story from only one part of the human past.

There's one particular interesting thing I discovered about the Incas and that city of theirs four miles up in the Andes. We, by that I mean our white brother, didn't discover this place until well into the 20th century. There's this stone wall in Machu Pichu that has faces of all the types of humans on the planet built into it. Even after the wearing down by the planet's wind force, the faces are still visible and recognizable. Now since the Incas didn't do the colonizing thing (dumb practice), how did they find out about all the types of humans on the planet to put them in that wall? Migration within our species accounts for a lot of variation and may be a partial answer to that wall. Even if the various cultures on this side of the planet were not directly related to each other, the fact that they shared similar knowledge indicates a common source of ideas.

So it appears that the ancestors of some of those people down south we now call Mexicans and my ancestors whom the Greeks called Egyptians must have gone to the same school, had the same parents and teachers, or something. They obviously learned their lessons well because the evidence of this similar knowledge and technology is still here with us today.

So, as I said at the outset of the essay, "Dude, I think we're related."

Everything is Tribal, not Racial

Racism, a negative emotion (energy wave) is aimed at another member of the same species who is not a member of one's own tribe. The older, non-Christian term tribal is more suited to this particular facet of human emotion.

All human group actions are tribal in nature—clubs, companies, both small and large, teams, associations, gangs (both the approved and the un-approved), congregations, cities, states, nations, etc., etc., etc. World Wars I and II were tribal wars between the same tribes of Europe (England, Germany and France), all aided by their various allies. Other tribes lost out during these two messy and expensive little ventures. Members of various other tribes that lived in the US at the time went to join the fight but their efforts were not really appreciated or acknowledged. Same thing even happened in the civil war this adolescent nation had recently and continues to fight to this very day. Lots of members of other tribes, both black and red, fought in that growth event but their efforts were not appreciated or honored.

In those white tribal wars, Poland was always the first to get invaded—what was that all about?

The tallest members of our species has this maniacal obsession of trying to wipe out one of the smallest family members; all the original Americans had their tribal enemies, a fact that prevented them joining forces and expelling the invading white tribes. Greeks and Turks have been arguing, over what I don't know, probably longer than the Judeans have been arguing amongst themselves. I really don't understand that thing between the Chinese and the Tibetans so I just classify it under tribalism. Wonder of wonders, it appears that the tribes of Ireland, calling themselves Protestant and Catholic, are actually going to try and find out why they've been at each others' throats all this time. Just how do they tell the difference? They all look alike, you know.

The longest continual tribal conflict in the family human that gets the most press is the sole domain of the Semitic tribes and their various manifestations. His-tory has recorded the destruction of the second Judean temple by the Romans.

Those hated Romans!!

Actually, running a vast empire requires a certain amount of order and the Romans just got pissed off about the constant tribal warfare in that part of their very busy and expensive empire. The same thing is going on over there today, but the Romans are long gone.

I know I'm tired of it; I'd take bets that the rest of the human family is tired of it, and some of the individual participants in that predictable drama are showing signs that they're even fed up with it, but tribalism rules.

As far as the Romans were concerned, running an empire required compromise and conciliation and, above all, practicality. The Romans would rather work with you than fight you. In their day, however, when it came to fighting them, they had the biggest stick. So they crushed yet another outbreak of tribalism and put an end to the constant foment that was prevalent in that part of their empire. The only remnant from their action is the Wailing Wall.

Sorry about that guys—chalk it up to tribalism.

That madness in what used to be Yugoslavia is another example of tribalism run amuck.

In our time, the type and focus of tribalism has been primarily from the colonizing tribes of Europe toward other members of the human family. These same concepts and practices were played out on the American stage and helped to create the now-dying American empire.

It really didn't last too long, did it?

Having had great sections of planetary history denied them, the tribes of Europe set forth re-discovering things that the rest of the human family had taken for granted, Concepts such as the earth being round, the movement of the stars and how to navigate using them, knowledge about magnets, the concept of the zero, the importance of bathing the body—such information had been denied the tribes of Europe by the church. That evolving organization devised a form of tribalism that insisted on converting others to their way of thinking, following their religious practices, adopting their standard of living and so on. Paramount in this new tribalism was the concept of white privilege. The planet is for us and we have the right to use it as we see fit.

Sound familiar?

It's all tribal.

Thud!!

The place is San Diego. California.

The time—our young country was slowly admitting that Vietnam was a horrible mistake and was beginning to pull out of that tiny place. It had never really been a threat to us anyway.

That whole thing was about rice.

After I was commissioned, the Navy sent me to an aircraft carrier to be part of ship's company. They were continuing the efforts of John Kennedy, and Harry Truman before him, to make the Navy look like the rest of the society. There had been very few black officers in that organization when I joined at the beginning of that ill-fated conflict.

As is the procedure in a military system, the worthiness of the individual is checked. A confidential clearance is almost a matter of routine. Once a person is commissioned as an officer or warrant officer, a secret clearance is an automatic procedure. It's only when one reaches a position that requires a top secret clearance that things slow down a bit.

I had reached that point in my brief naval career.

While in the Hospital Corps School at Great Lakes, the Navy discovered that I had a four year degree and offered me the opportunity to go to OCS. At the time, I expressed the interest in a commission in the Medical Service Corps. By then, I had almost two years service in the medical branch. I was working in medical research at the time and thought it would great to be commissioned and work in an area that was familiar to me. It seemed a logical step to me. However, when I accepted the offer, I was sent to Newport, RI. There I was to become a junior officer of the line. This is the largest section of the Navy. All other parts serve it. I was to eventually learn that during those days, the MSC branch of the Navy was a bit more prejudiced than was the larger general Navy. They really didn't want too many black officers.

So, after my adventures in Newport, RI came to an end, I went to the West Coast to join my ship. It was aboard this vessel that certain events occured that led to my separation from the Navy and it was centered around that top-secret clearance I mentioned. By the time the bureaucratic wheels of the separation process began, the carrier to which I was assisgned had been refitted and had returned to her home port of San Diego. We had spent 11½ months in Bremerton, WA. She was soon to depart for Yankee Station in the South China Sea. I was not with them when they left. Later on I was to realize that this had been a blessing in disguise.

While waiting for those bureaucratic wheels to turn, I literally had nothing to do. I was assigned to an officer's barracks at the 32nd Street Naval Station. Without a duty assignment, I was a free agent, so to speak.

Realizing that I would eventually be on my own, I secured an apartment in the Hillcrest section of San Diego. At the time it was one of the sections of that seaport city where major illegal drug sales were taking place. It was also very pretty and typically American and very white. Well kept lawns and neat houses were the order of the day. However, it was some time before I learned of these secrets about my newly chosen neighborhood.

During my free-agent status, which lasted several months, I made acquaintance with several people who hung out at a jazz-disco bar in downtown San Diego. There were about five people in this partying gang. We would close the bars in San Diego at 2 a.m. and then go south of the border to Tiajuana to continue partying. Since they don't actually "close" their bars there (they don't have the American hangup about alcohol), we would generally stay there until 6 a.m or so and then come back to San Diego to continue in the first bars that were open after the American alcohol curfew had been lifted.

On this particular day, I had not gone down south as usual, but stayed at home. I left the house around 11 a.m. I went over on University Avenue to a Jack-in-the-Box and had an early lunch. My favorite sandwich then was the BonusBurger. They don't serve that one anymore.

After my lunch, I went to a bar on the opposite corner from the hamburger place. There were two other patrons at the bar when I walked in, a woman and a man. Both were white humans, as was the bartender. I walked to an open spot and sat at the bar with the others. The woman was to my left on the other side of the bar break and the man was three stools to my right. I ordered a Bohemia and a glass.

Halfway through my beer, the bartender asked the male patron if he wanted another drink. When he posed this question, he addressed the gentlemen by his name. He was, apparently, a regular.

"Would you like another, Mr. MacAtee"? He said "Yes".

That name was part of my family tree on my mother's side.

I inquired of the gentlemen if he had relatives in the state of Kentucky. He replied "Yes". "Anywhere near the Fort Knox area"?, I continued. "Why yes", he said. I informed him that my maternal grandmother's maiden name was MacAtee and she was from that part of Kentucky.

"Who was your grandmother", came his next question?

I answered, "Bettye". He then said, "She married John E.?"

"Yes".

"Well, that was my mother's sister."

I don't remember the reaction from the woman at the bar or even if there was one, but that sound you just heard was the bartender's jaw hitting the floor.

I was to eventually relay the details of this event to one of the griots of my family. That's an African term for those of you don't already know. All human families were, at one time, practitioners of the oral tradition. Events and records of the tribe were kept in the minds of certain individuals. When data is stored in this fashion, it can't be edietied or tampered with by outsiders. Our species left this behind when we were told the written word was the way to go.

Yeh, right!!!

In my family, one of these was my mother's older sister. She knew immediately who that man at the bar was. "Oh, that's was Frank, your grandmother's sister's oldest boy. He went to California some years ago and, by all accounts, is doing well."

I never saw him again. My life was soon to take some very interesting and unusual turns but, as they say, that's another story.

Class Dismissed

I can't even remember what part of that year it was,
but I have come to realize that I can let the reader
locate this event along our common time line in this realm.

This unscheduled little class took place in what is presently called the San Fernando Valley. I hear tell that at one time is was called the Valley of Smoke by those who lived there first. I guess those people would visit but figured it was better not to stay. The smoke is much more mobile these days and never seems to go away. Human mobility is what put us at the location where this brief class was held.

Joe, the instructor, was a little tall for his age, probably 14 or 15. He was being held in one of the housing units near the bottom of the hill. The youngest inmate boys were housed in the units at the top of the hill, and as you came down the hill the ages of the inhabitants increased. He would have been labeled a Vato (low rider/gang member) that had come from one of the numerous Valley communities. In fact, most of the kids in this juvenile facility were from the northwestern section of the City of the Angels. Joe had not yet committed totally to the gang philosophy but he was nibbling around the edges, so to speak. He had stolen a car for joyriding, got caught and was doing his first stint.

Part of Joe's nose architecture was not standard from his beginning—he had a deviated septum—a rather fragile one, in his case. On more than one occasion we had to cart him off to the nearest hospital to make sure that the bleeding had stopped. Those little capillaries in that very thin dividing bone would rupture during his sleep causing blood to collect where it shouldn't. On this particular night, the task of escorting him fell to me. We arrived at the hospital emergency room somewhere near the middle of the graveyard shift. The resident medical priest is out making rounds, so after the registration procedure was finished, the admitting nurse asked us to have a seat in the waiting room.

Take a chill pill.

As has come to be custom in our land, wherever and whenever citizens are hanging around, and sometimes *left* hanging while these bureaucracies overcome their inbred inertia, we sat down to the omnipresence of the tube. The following is the scene that was in play when Joe turned his attention to the eye in the sky:

An old man with a full white beard, dressed in what appeared to be the garb of an Islamic cleric and his head bound in a dark-colored turban, is descending the stairs of a ramp that has been rolled up to a rather large jet plane. At the bottom of the stairs is a sizeable crowd of people, which surrounds the bottom of the ramp and stretches along the length of the plane in both directions. Immediately next to the bottom step of the ramp is a small collection of men, of varying ages, garbed similarly as is the old man—some of the turbans were light in color and others was dark. The announcer is informing the television audience that the old man has just landed after returning from political exile in France. As the narrator continues, the camera pans along the length of the crowd next to the airplane. As we continue to hear the description of this scene and the events that led up to the arrival and return of this old man, the camera begins to swing its attention beyond the plane and the crowd enclosing it. The camera slowly moves its view beyond the events at the jet plane, to another large crowd of people a short distance away, shouting as loudly as the first crowd. However, this crowd was being contained behind a very long fence. Apparently the people in this second crowd were not pleased with the arrival of that old man coming down the steps and were protesting his arrival. The noise from the crowd behind the fence has now drowned out the sound of the crowd at the plane.

As we are watching this new scene, a great cheer is suddenly heard from the crowd out of sight of the camera, which now turns quickly in time to see the old man put his foot on the earth. He motions to one of the other clerics who helps him to kneel and kiss the earth. The commentator stops talking and the camera follows the steps of the old cleric, amid much tumult, as he takes his first steps toward his destiny.

Suddenly, the silence is broken by Joe's voice. "Hell, that ain't nothing but a couple of gangs."

Class dismissed.

It's a Male Thing

Civilization, as we've all come to understand this on-going process, is a male concept.

Before he left us, Joseph Campbell told us that males are concerned with ***doing*** and females are concerned with ***being***. Quite a difference here, yes?

Just look at the various religious laws and customs aimed at reducing the influence of the female of our species. Interesting set of conditions we have here.

We've managed to set up a system that denigrates or otherwise belittles the very member of the species whose job it is to produce the species, of which all of us are a part, including the male aspect.

So any philosophy, credo, religion or body of thought that belittles, eliminates, subjugates, diverts energy from or otherwise denies the existence of the female for purposes other than those designed for the male, is essentially out of balance, confused, contradictory, off-base and lost.

Besides, that idea of a male god creating life probably started with the Greeks or some other tribal mythology from that same time zone. Zeus gave birth to his daughter, Athena, from his forehead, fully armored even. Now that was a real migrane!

The Romans, being the practical types they were, just picked up everything the Greeks had left, rounded off all the edges and moved on.

The Babylonians, whose stories make up MAJOR portions of the Old Testament in the original bible, had other examples of the creation as well.

So when the Hebrews that left Egypt got around to telling the rest of us about their adventures, they didn't tell us about the Egyptian creation story. They told their own tribal story, which is mostly Greek, not mine. Theirs was centered about the male aspect.

Mine wasn't.

The creation story of Kemet (Egypt is a white tribal term) involves a primeval mud—from dust thou art and to dust thou shall return. In addition, the Hebrew story of the birth of the son of God (Jesus) was already being told in Egypt before they left, but the names were different. Those names were Isis, Horus, Osiris and Set. Whereas the story of the male offspring of a supreme being was not new, the Hebrew version made a few changes to the basic storyline.

The story of the birth of the son of God (Horus) from the Kemetian standpoint goes generally as follows:

Set, the brother to Osiris (the male aspect) tricked him into laying in a sarcophagus whereupon he cut up the body and distributed it throughout the land. Isis (the female aspect) traveled throughout the land and collected all the various body parts and re-assembled the body of her husband/brother (male aspect). The only part not found was the phallus; (penis is the modern term). She lay upon the re-assembled body and BEGAT Horus, the son of God.

*This is the origin of the birth
of the son of a god
without the sexual act.*

This tribal story from my people is common throughout the human family. The Hebrew version is just another way of telling the same story. However, the emphasis was shifted to the male aspect only.

The fact that Mary, a human female, was chosen was not new either. Male gods coming to earth to woo mortal females was routine. Zeus was constantly appearing on earth in order to produce offspring. He would appear as a shower of silver rain, sometimes as a bull (the ancient symbol of power) and sometimes as a tree. These offspring were all called half-or demigods—part human and part god. There was no sexism in the pre-Christian stories. Even the female gods would come to earth to produce offspring with human males–demigods from the distaff side.

After the church got its act together, they set about creating saints or *more-than-human* individuals (demigods). After a lengthy analysis of the person's life and checking out of miracles or great works performed by these individuals, they are made into saints. It's the males of the church that get together and decide these things.

Are there any female cardinals in the Catholic Church? I don't think so. If there were, would they be called cardinalettes?

It's the males who will elect the next pope.

It's definitely a male thing.

At Year's End

We all know a lot of things in this time are broken and don't work
We'd really like to fix them, but nobody seems to know how
There are many who tell us about those parts really messed up
Like the price of that white liquid we drink, taken from the cow.

Emotions often run high when we talk about how and what to do
To put an end to what we all feel are the great rip-offs of all time
Class action lawsuits get good press but don't do the job so well
Of setting things straight, promote good feelings and peace of mind.

There are those who think that blowing things up is the way to go
To fix what they see as a wrong, to set the record right for us all
However, most in our local family know this thinking to be flawed
And wisely turn away from the words of the violent male's angry call.

Every year 'bout this time, we celebrate the idea of peace and love
That, we tell ourselves, is the real essence of our existence here
We hear retold the story of a gift from a creator in the great above
To show us the way out of ignorance, prejudice and programmed fear.

What most fail to recognize is that change creates its own life-pattern
And using old and outdated thought styles doesn't work anymore
Most don't see the cycles of life as they pass through us all here
And there is no grand record-keeper tallying up your mortal score.

As the human family becomes more and more unto itself as one
The ideas of separateness and apartness begin to slowly fade and die
The violence that we now see is the last gasp of a bankrupt system
Built on manufactured human differences and a made-up social lie.

This cycle of a thousand years is not all that important as we been told
There are other cycles of which we all should heed and become aware
These are the cycles of the planet upon which we all depend and need
These the cycles of the earth, the waters, above and below, and the air.

It is time we pay heed to the life of the living being that controls us all
That pays no mind to the male perspective with its bombast and speed
Planetary cycles are of much greater times, longer than those we use
She has no thought of human tribulations and the male-driven greed.

So in this time of our own cyclical renewal, let us begin to hear and see
The real aspect of life as was intended for us eons before these days
Reach back into your own tribal memories to learn of our joined past
To regain our collective oneness and the balanced human life-ways.

Richmond–1998

One Hemlock Cocktail, please—Shaken not Stirred.

In a time when we are debating the right of the state to continue killing members of our society "officially", it becomes necessary to discuss how we came to this sorry state of affairs.

Capital punishment, in and of itself, is something that has been a part of human history for millennia. Apparently, the Kemetians used poisons and such; Cleopatra used one of these ancient practices on herself at the end. The Greeks made Socrates drink that tea of the hemlock plant—deadly stuff in strong concentrations—Ouzo gets its kick from the same plant. Those Greek guys who gave that particular capital punishment order—a bunch of frustrated Republicans…claimed that man was "corrupting the morals of young males under his tutelage."

Those Roman dudes used the battle sword in meting out the death order in military cases. The small personal sword was dusted off when the order was to be carried out by the offender. This same personal sword was also taken up in cases of "political capital punishment", as illustrated by that little thing with Caesar, the Julius variety. The two Gracci brothers met their deaths at the hand of a "senatorial mob", as described by one historian. These two men were like the Kennedy brothers of our time—wanted to enact laws to do weird stuff like land reform—that is, giving land back to the people that had owned it originally but had it purloined from them by members of the senate. A few well-placed dagger holes put an end to such nonsense, ergo, political capital punishment.

However, it wasn't until the early Christians begin to organize their efforts that we saw really creative methods of capital punishment. As the Christian era got under way, the church began to turn out the intellectual lights in all the human minds it controlled. Ancient knowledge such as mathematics, architecture, science—the essential tools for running a civilization practically and efficiently—went by the wayside, was shunned and made into something evil. One of the last teachers of the ancient wisdom was a woman named Hypatia. Her father was a great teacher and philosopher. She continued in his footsteps and when she refused to stop teaching the old stuff, she was dragged into the city square, by monks no less, and killed by having her skin scrapped off with seashells.

Hollywood, eat your heart out!!!!

After the Catholic Church really got going, they came up with the Iron Maiden—that chest with all those sharp spikes on both the door and the chest itself. The thing stood upright and when the poor soul who was doomed was put inside—you get the picture.

Capital punishment by torture was quite popular in the latter part of the first millennium and into the first part one we just left. There were three degrees of torture—that's where we get the first, second and third degree thing in our time—it's a holdover from the days of torture. If we are to believe information as put forth in the movies, then the Catholic Church did indeed send assassins to England to kill Elizabeth I, only they got caught and met their fate by torture. We're still doing it in our time, mostly by secret people like the CIA, the FBI and various police departments, but we lie to ourselves, especially white folk, that it's not happening and we pretend horror when knowledge of such activity comes to light.

In the past, by the time the third degree tools and techniques were dragged out, everyone had either confessed or died. You were really lucky if you died.

Beheading was all the rage for a considerable period of time, especially in both England and France. During the Terror (known affectionately as the French Revolution), capital punishment became a sort of entertainment. All other forms of commerce occurred during the "loping-off-of-heads". Food was sold, pockets were picked, pictures were drawn and sold (pre-Kodak) and souvenirs were sold as well. The Terror lasted for three years.

Odd little thing about the guillotine, that heavy duty razor blade that a clever man in France came up with. He petitioned the reigning king of the day to use his invention. It sounded like a good idea to Louis 13th and he granted the maker a commission. Money was made by all connected with the manufacture of this invention. However, Louis lived long enough to regret his previous act—this new fangled gadget was used to lop off his head eventually during that Terror I talked about in the paragraph right before this one.

The British, on the other hand, stayed with the ax and sword. I believe the sword was reserved for special cases and the ax used primarily in the majority of cases, or it might have been the other way around. The last public execution in England was that of a 13-year-old girl who had stolen a loaf of bread to feed her infant child. She handed the baby to a spectator as she went to her death by hanging.

Burning at the stake, another cute form of Christian capital punishment, is more familiar to those of us living in the United States—it was something that happened in our own his-story. The English burned witches as well and, in doing so, used faggots of wood to carry out the sentence (bundles of long and slender tree branches tied together to make a tossable bundle of wood). Over here in the new world, the guys in New England actually hanged more people accused of being witches (mostly women–same story as in Europe), but there were a few that were torched.

After the gun appeared, death by firing squad became an honorable death for those living the military life. That particular invention opened up news methods of doing ourselves in.

Places where the Christians didn't get a foothold had their own methods of maintaining the status quo. The Arabs had an interesting public execution device. It was an expanded and greatly enlarged version of the personal knife that was worn by them. In that part of the world, drawing and quartering (having your limbs tied to four different horses who were driven away in four different directions) was a technique used sometimes. Sounds particularly messy. Usually, the poor victim's body had to be hacked at the joints because the horses could never quite pull of the act totally. We've all heard about the water torture those guys over in China used and the best example I've seen of that Japanese act of self immolation was in a movie called Shogun. The WWII name of hari kari is not the correct name for that ritual, however. Something got lost in the translation

Apparently the Hawaiians used that war club of theirs on that Cooke fellow when they realized he wasn't what they first thought he was. Ouch!!!

In our time, the good Christians at Westinghouse were thinking up the electric chair. Old Sparky is still here, but it's in a museum somewhere. This is one electrical gadget that Thomas of the Edison variety didn't think up. It seems that Westinghouse beat him to the patent office on this one.

Hanging has been around since day one and in and of itself, is not too dramatic, as styles go. However, it can be done at a moments notice. Just look into the history of the South and the use of hanging in the public lynchings. Blacks, primarily males, were hanged and burned routinely because of the fear of blacks that whites still can't explain.

As our chemical knowledge has increased, the additional methods of execution have appeared with this new knowledge. The gas chamber is a direct result of an accident that demonstrated the killing potential of hydrogen cyanide.

Eventually the drug companies got in on the act. Poisons and substances of this nature are essentially chemicals, things these guys play around with all the time. Arsenic was a favorite until detection methods made it possible for the forensic guys to find it. However, individuals usually employed it when they wanted to get rid of competition or ex-lovers.

The debate is now about the use of the death penalty, using assorted means, as employed by the various states that make up this present political system. It appears that the US is still the leader in the use of capital punishment, i.e., death at the hands of the state.

The word justice is often used when sentences are meted out to those citizens who have transgressed some capital law. In actuality, justice is never served in this manner. Only the act of revenge is served in these cases. Justice is best served by prevention.

So in our time we see the death penalty handed out to mostly poor people, a greater number of them being brown and/or black. It's part of that fear of poverty that my white brother has in his brain.

Can someone tell me why the needle site is sterilized when giving the injection to carry out the death penalty?

Every Soil is A Brave Man's Country

From the beginning man is dust,
when he's living, he's flesh and blood
when he dies he returns to the dust and the sea stirs up the mud.

Up to the shore of the sea I come
my back to the sheltered land
my gaze ever to the open sea, my feet mired in the solid sand.

I yearn to go, yet long to stay
in this land I know so well
my heart is on the vast green sea but my bones won't rot in hell.

In hell, I say—is here on Earth
in this land of plenty, and free—
the plenty is mostly prejudice and hate and very free of quality.

But what of all the other lands
are there any free and just—
does peace abide here anywhere, is there such a word as trust?

The tide is in, I feel its breath, now lapping at my feet
with arms outstretched, I welcome thee
death is tasteless, but sweet.

Santa Monica
1971

Sprit and Non-sprit—Corporeal and Non-corporeal

The life force—that non-physical part of us all—is just that, **NOT** physical. It can't be analyzed, quantified, typed, categorized or labeled. Once any attempt is made to identify or quantify the creative, non-physical portion of our existence, one runs immediately into problems with the naming procedure.

I was once confronted (actually threatened) by a Christian zealot. I guess I had said something that made him want to save me. Toward the end of our conversation he said it was "my last chance for him to save me." This poor child didn't even know that the word Allah was the Arabic word for God. And, we all know what Christians have been doing to Moslems lo these many centuries and vice versa.

On the other hand, the original guys on this side of the planet, the folks we call Chinese and those guys in live in a land called India, the original inhabitants of the land we now call Australia, all had different, yet similar, ideas about the spirit body within us.

Check this out—those aborigines (that's a colonial term) in the land down under, tell us of a time referred to as the "dream time". Apparently during this period of our ancient past, all the creatures of the earth communicated with each other. What a concept—Dr. Doolittle does it too.

It is widely accepted in today's adolescent American culture that those original Americans embodied spirit into everything. The early missionaries regarded such concepts as pagan and termed it idolatry or some such nonsense. Once you accept as fact the practice and belief that the planet is yours to exploit in order to maintain your standard of living and not give back to that same planet, you arrive at the place we find ourselves today.

Depleted spirit.

Spirit embodied everything prior to the Christian era. The original ritual practice of wicca was spirit based, attributing spirit to all levels of existence, quite similar to the philosophy of the original Americans. Wicca is also both male and female based.

As different ideas replaced older ones, these spirit concepts were forgotten and a focus on the purely physical was put in their place.

Since spirit is non-physical, it does not obey the laws of our physical world. Quantum physics is of no value here. Those rules don't apply. Time does not apply. Just talk to any medium who speaks with those who have passed on. There are several with us here today who display these ancient talents, talents that were suppressed by the church and made into something evil and to be avoided. These individuals are also telling us something many refuse to believe that this ability to communicate with the spirits of those who have left the physical world is something that is native to our species. WE ALL HAVE IT!

America produced an outstanding talent in the form of a man named Edgar. He slept while he was passing along information from the non-physical world, which exists here with us. Since the non-corporeal body exists outside the concept of time, it easily sees events we would physically identify as from the future. Mr. Edgar saw that our adolescent nation would undergo considerable physical change (as in land mass changes) during the early part of this present millennium. He also told us there would be continued existence after these changes.

Other members of our species who are even older tell us of life cycles. According to those pyramid builders down south of here, we are coming to the end of the Fourth Cycle and entering the Fifth Cycle. These cycles have to do with spiritual growth and not physical growth. The intellect of our species has largely been directed toward the manipulation of the physical continuum for the past two thousand years. Now that we realize that there is more than the physical, our search for information about the non-physical, which was here in the past, is being sought for by more and more of us.

Searching for spiritual information is best done by each individual, at his or her own pace. Be forewarned that no other member of our species can lead you to where you understand your part in all of this, your part in both the physical and the non-physical. Do not follow leaders. They can't lead. The spirit speaks to us all individually and when it is necessary. Some of us don't hear because we've been distracted. The happiness of an individual in this drama is best determined by the particular individual in question. If you see others you wish to emulate, do so, but in your own style. If you don't see others you wish to emulate, then set your own course. Your part of the spirit knows what's best for you.

Learn to trust it.

Un-organized Religion

Organized religion is an oxy-moron, a contradiction in terms.

A brief glance at the history of the white tribes of Europe gives you hundreds of years of disorganization brought about by the church and its rampant tribalism. Once the church picked up the pieces of the collapsed Roman Empire, they didn't have the ability to operate anything that complex, so various factions began competing for local and regional control.

> *It is imperative that we all come to the realization that the entire purpose and direction of western religion was and still is the acquisition of land and mineral wealth.*

The Greeks and Romans were much more honest in this respect. After the Romans took over things at the death of Alexander, they set about organizing their system and did an amazing job, even by today's standards. City planning originated with them. It only took the church and those it controlled several hundred years to rediscover this fact.

Here's what essentially happened because of un-organized religion.

In order to set itself up in business, the church found it necessary to discredit all religious practices, knowledge and belief systems that had existed prior to its arrival. This meant that anything from Egypt, Greece and Rome had to be wiped away from the minds of anyone they could convince. Such an action required war and lots of it. So much war came about that as a result, we now have two forms of Christianity on our planet up to the present time.

It is interesting to note that the present pope just recently visited the headquarters of that other Christianity for the first time in hundreds of years.

> **They've been at each others throats all this time.**

This destruction of previous planetary knowledge is how the black tribes became non-people in the eyes of whites. All knowledge, scientific, mathematical and architectural that the Greeks and Romans developed had its origins in Kemet, the nation the Greeks called Egypt. Euclid, the father of geometry, spent over 15 years of his life in Egypt studying that body of knowledge known as "The Mysteries". Freemasonry was an attempt by those members of the suppressed white tribes to reconnect with this body of human knowledge.

The dominance of Egyptian thought and practices was so strong, the early Coptic Christians decided to burn the Alexandrian library to destroy the influence of this very dominating culture. They then proceeded to steal rather liberally from the Egyptian rituals and practices. Take a look at the miter that the Roman Catholic Pope wears. It's one of the two crowns that the Pharaoh wore in the performance of his royal duties. The second part of the pharaoh's crown with that serpent had to go, however.

> **When the Pharaoh wore**
> **both the miter and the serpent on his head,**
> **he was representing**
> **both the lower and upper parts**
> **of his kingdom simultaneously.**

So the Adam and Eve creation story was used to discredit that ancient symbol of wisdom and the poor reptile has suffered ever since. The incense thing that's used in Orthodox, Roman Catholic, Anglican and Episcopalian masses comes directly from the temples of Egypt. A visit to the Cairo of today will show the visitor examples of the original Egyptian rituals, plus all those that followed, Coptic, Catholic, Islam and Judaism. They're all there today!!!

Even ancient Roman holidays were pressed into service to fit the new Christian order. The central character of the bible, Jonah (Jesus, Jeremiah, Joseph and all other names are representations of the same character—the hero) was an Aquarius. When asked how the messiah would be recognized, he is reported to have said "Go to the gates of the city; there you will find a waterbearer. Follow him."

The sign of Aquarius is the waterbearer.

In order to take advantage of the people's habit of gathering for the old Roman holidays, those days were subsumed to serve a new purpose. The ancient holiday of the Saturnalia (December 25 was one of the days in this occurrence that lasted a couple of weeks) was used by the early church to "get out the word". That mistake is still with us, particularly here in this country. Elsewhere on the planet, the birth of Jonah is celebrated in January.

It's definitely not organized.

As stated previously, the sole focus of organized religion was and is the acquisition of land and mineral wealth. When Rome went broke, the church had to go were the money was and that was in Istanbul where ancient trade routes converged. There's lots of human activity going on up there—people doing what comes naturally for our species—TRADE AND COMMERCE. So this Constantine dude goes up that way, finally gets up enough troops to take over and eventually builds up enough capital to go back south to Rome where he wanted to be in the first place. There the one form of the Christian church sits to this day. It was extremely bloody and unorganized.

Along the way, this other body of religious thought shows up. It's called Islam. It arose in the same part of the world. There are elements of the Egyptian religion buried inside Islam as well. The origins of this philosophy are well known and documented as is the life of its primary prophet. He's buried in Mecca in that fabulous black tomb (sarcopha-gus—sound familiar)?? However, we don't have such data about the central prophet of the other competing religion.

Americans tend to call all other bodies of thought religions. This is a huge mistake. Many other members of our species do a much better job of living or putting into practice their belief systems. There are considerably less conflicts recorded between the other systems followed by various members of our human family.

Americans also mistakenly refer to the Japanese practice of Shinto as a state religion. Nothing could be farther from the truth. As the Japanese came in contact with additional members of the human family, they adopted portions of each tribe's belief system that they found attractive or logical. The practice of Shinto evolved with them and remains there today despite the relentless onslaught of ignorant American evangelists to "convert" the Japanese to Christianity. Hindus have been practicing their belief system longer than Christians, as has the home-grown ethos of China called Daoism. There's Buddhism which spread alongside Christianity in many places and remains one of human family systems.

A closer look at all of these "systems" reveals a similarity and "likeness of approach to things spiritual" that comes with being human. There is no one correct way to deal with this part of our existence in this realm-never has been, never will be.

Essentially, as it is practiced in this country at this time, the religious ethic is one of deep-seeded insecurity. Modern evangelicals are constantly taking religious barometric readings to gauge the religious pressure, as it were. Consequently, many feel the need to ask other members of our species if "they believe in God".

At the outset, this is an insufferably rude question, but typical of the colonial and Protestant ethic that curses our nation to this day. One's belief in one's own concept of a higher power is probably THE MOST SACRED AND PRIVATE thought each of us has. It is even more private and sacred than our concept of loyalty to the country of origin and all that entails.

So to have total strangers coming up to you, waving the most recently revised edition of this excessively edited book, and offering to "save your soul" indicates the level of disorganization that exists in this ethos to this very day.

SEX
and the
Single, Married, Divorced,
Recently Separated or
Reconciled Person

Hugh Hefner said it best: "America has two big hang ups—sex and money".

The question is, just what America was he talking about when he made this prophetic statement during the early days of his empire?

He was talking about white boys—WASPs, Catholics, Jews, Gentiles and all other subsets of the white male population that went to his Playboy Clubs from the beginning to the end of that bit of planetary his-story.

There were very few males of color that went to these places routinely-as entertainers, yes, but very few males of color went to the clubs to ogle the white females that paraded around in those very brief bunny costumes.

Can't have black males looking at white females. We used to hang and burn black boys routinely here when they were suspected of looking at a white female. It was a matter of sport, you know—because American white boys have this sexual insecurity they don't recognize.

Don't you dare look at a white female.
I can produce as many slaves as I want
with the black or brown female,
but you can't even look at my woman.
I'll kill you if you do.

By today's standards, what Hefner offered was mild. We've become desensitized to the female form (the curse of Eve) and it's all the white boy's doing. Black boys diss their women because they've been dissed by the white boy. As said in the Navy, "Shit flows down hill."

Betty Davis said it best when she observed that the female form has been washed, prodded, douched and talked about on American television to no end. Oddly enough, we are just now beginning to discuss things physical about the male form. It has also be noted that with all the medical problems and mysteries confronting this vast pharmaceutical system we've developed, what did they come up with—something to grow hair and keep the penis erect. We're talking about those white boys again.

The level of the "hangup" was indicated when George Carlin told us that most white boys got their first glimpse of the naked female form by looking at National Geographic. Apparently it was alright to look at nude black and brown females whom the white male has always considered sub-human but not the white female.

The white boys had to pay dearly to get close to a female, even if he was married. Vicarious fantasizing was permitted in these Playboy clubs, but the actual contact between the male and the female was taboo of the first order as directed by the church.

Meeting your sexual needs was okay, but don't get caught. It's okay for the male to "sow his wild oats"—heaven forbid that a female should enjoy sex—she's a harlot, a whore. Stone her, lock her up, but let him go.

As my godson would say, "That's messed up".

The tragedy of that dis-organized religion I mentioned earlier was the destruction of all tribal rituals related to the education of our species about the importance of birth control and reproductive responsibility.

Once the sexual side of our existence became "dirty and sinful", anything that had to do with birth control, the prevention of unwanted pregnancies, the power of the female form and her self-control over these functions, came under the control of the male.

That dis-organized religion is a male thing. Females were added to the religious hierarchy almost as an afterthought—an implied apology to the slaughter of females throughout the white tribes' planetary history. The majority of the witches burned during the heyday of the inquisition were female. It was another land grab. Go search the legal records of many European nations. The data is there. Single females who owned land were a threat to the sexually frustrated males that set up the church system. Their original knowledge about the birth process, something males are not designed for, was a direct threat to the power and authority over the increasing wealth that was accumulating with the increase in trade.

When those dissatisfied Hebrews left my tribe's land, they took the concept of non-sexual birth and used it in the Mary and Jesus story. Mind you, the non-sexual birth process story is found as far back as Sumer, way before a lot of other cultures got started. So after the church got their hands on that same story, the sexual reproduction of our species (*the same process used by most life forms on this planet*) became something sinful and totally "of man" and to be despised. Since we had to bear children because of Eve's "sin", the female became the object of the male's fear and hate. It was codified into religious ritual and we have the mess and attitudes that persist to this day.

HANG-UP OF THE FIRST MAGNITUDE!!!!

Let's Go Get Stoned

—says the line in that song Ray Charles did a while back. I do believe other musicians covered it as well, but I remember his version more than any other. He might have even written it.

We teach each other with music.

At that time, the number of substances that one could ingest to "go get stoned" was somewhat smaller than what we see these days. More people, greater variety of things used to "get stoned". That's a no-brainer. As long we have been sentient, humans have been taking things to "go get stoned"—alter the conscious state.

We pay millions of dollars for artwork painted on the left bank of Paris in the 18th Century depicting citizens drinking a substance called Absinthe. The Greeks have this drink called Uzo. Like Absinthe, it's has hallucinogenic properties. My home state is known planet-wide for the alcoholic drink it makes—those vast limestone deposits and caves spread all over the place filter the natural ground water. This pure water becomes the basis for Kentucky Bourbon and the Tennessee Sippin' Whiskeys.

Talk to your grandparents and great grandparents about the patent medicines we used to take all over the planet. Pure unadulterated morphine, opium and belladonna, suspended in alcohol. No wonder the decade between 1890 and 1900 was called the "gay nineties." Everybody was whacked out of their gourds.

My ancestors used beer as payment to their citizens for their service in building those pyramids. The Mayans made a beer from chocolate which was reserved, oddly enough, for the royals. The Russians make a marvelous drink called vodka. I believe the potato is the basis for this liquid. In addition to making all sorts of things from rice plant, the Japanese make that saki from the same plant. It's usually served warm. Every culture of our species has something that it uses to alter the consciousness after the work of the day—it's part of being human.

So what's all this static and bombast I hear in my young country these days? Why has drugs become such a hot topic in America recently?

Personally, I think it has to do with the way we practice capitalism.

An example to illustrate this concept is the plant called cannabis. Since this particular plant only became illegal in 1937, the prohibition against it relatively recent. At present, more money is being made with this product being classified as illegal than would be if it were legal. Making paper from this plant would change that economic picture instantly. The people of Kemet were the first humans to make paper and they used the papyrus that grew alongside that river that was vital to them. The wasp also makes a type of paper when they build their homes. Silly, short-sighted white boys, for the most part, are still cutting down trees for paper.

Many movie and television writers' careers are peppered with stories about the evils of this cannabis plant and other Schedule I members. Billions of dollars have been paid to advertise other products whose manufacturers sponsor popular media entertainment letting us see the good guys win and snuff out the "bad drug dealer". Hollywood is into this subject <u>big time</u>—Oscars have been won with such stories.

In the case of that cannabis plant, it was one of several plants used widely by the colonial powers when they started their empires. Jute, sisal and hemp were the natural fibers used to make all the ropes that made it possible for all those ships go sailing all around our planet.

When Dupont discovered nylon in 1937, they saw the potential for using this new fiber for everything imaginable. When we all went through that polyester thing back in the 70s, it was their attempt to eliminate cotton as the fiber of choice. We soon found out that this was not such a good idea. 100% polyester fiber holds body odors and stains until the end of time.

The creases looked fabulous but
nobody wanted to sit next to you.

Fibers of lesser import were not as lucky. Hemp, jute and sisal were doomed. About the same time, our very young nation decided that it *did* want to go home and have a beer, a glass of whiskey or wine after work. So the prohibition movement had the winds taken out of its sails. A lot of the proponents of prohibition had to find a new cause that could generate income, so they looked around for a new evil to condemn.

There sits that other use for the hemp plant. Taking a cue from William Randolph Hearst, great lies were used to create a fear in the mind of the populace and, as they say, the rest is his-story.

Fear was a tactic used for centuries
by the Catholic Church
on the tribes of Europe.

Since non-European tribal descendants were not really the targets for this anti-cannabis propaganda campaign, the tactic worked. In addition, non-whites were soon classified as the purveyors of this evil and the legal system was turned against them.

Presently, those directing this "war on drugs" are making money on so many different levels that it boggles the mind. Vast amounts of assets from land to the very substances themselves have been "seized" in this war. All this means is that the wealth created by these substances has merely changed hands. At the same time, we continue to write new and more dramatic stories about these substances in their "illegal" status and continue to point that crooked accusatory finger at the wrong guy.

"Show me the money" and I'll show you the forces behind it all. Mr. Carlin has told us that if we as a nation really wanted to put an end to these substances and their presence here, we'd arrest those with the most money. Since the most money resides in our banking system, we're not about to touch these guys.

The "old money" in one of our oldest American cities was made by selling Opium to the citizens of China shortly after the end of our un-civil war. Once we admit that alcohol is a drug and call it such, then we will have to admit that the Kennedy family's wealth was first obtained by selling a drug. Aristotle Oasis' profession as a seller of "Turkish tobacco" was widely known outside America. He had such dealings with other high members of this society, including the brother of FDR. Before his death, silly America worshipped Oasis because he was wealthy beyond anyone's wildest dreams.

The occasional arrest or assassination of a "major" drug dealer who's black or brown, and the continued pointing of that crooked accusatory finger is no longer sufficient and is simply a smoke screen and a lie.

Drugs, legal and/or illegal, are an essential and critical part of the economy of this nation. Once we admit this to ourselves, it will cease to be a problem. Legalize the Schedule I items and tax them. The taboo will have been removed and the demand will go down. Those of you with children know if you forbid something and don't explain your reasons, the object or action forbidden will soon show up.

Besides, as a previous Los Angeles police chief once said, "As long as white America believed that evil drugs were something brown and black people used, it was not a problem. As soon as white America found out its own children were doing drugs, it suddenly became a problem."

The "problem" is not in Mexico, it's not in Nicaragua, it never was in Colombia and it's certainly not in Iran or the highlands of South America. The "problem" is here.

As the Arcade de Tijuana said during the Nixon administration: "You gringos stop buying, we'll stop selling".

Could someone please get me a cold Tuborg in the green bottle?

A Borrowed Line

Looking for heroes, searching all day,
leaders can't lead you, that path's the wrong way.

Choosing another to make things all right
is like stopping with wind or cursing the night

A city full of leaders is backwards, at best
they're all climbing to status and scared like the rest.

Looking for heroes, searching forever,
leaders won't lead you, they can't do it, never.

Your world is all you have and the leader is you
and the man who says he'll lead you is playing you for the fool.

So don't believe all those promises every four years or so,
because leaders can never deliver and this we all know.

Looking for heroes, futile players to the sky,
leader don't lead you, they all fade by and by.

Controlling your own world makes the whole thing a little better,
for leadership worship is just another fetter.

Just leave control of my life up to me, and
we both will end up happy, just you wait and see.

Don't look for heroes, and leaders will never do,
A hero's just a sandwich, and the leader has always been you.

Sylmar
1981

Such a Special Place?

In my white brother's written and oral history, there are many accounts of his belief in his version of the 'end of time' and the so-called final outcome or the ultimate fate of our species. Other family members also have stories about the end of time or the end of the earth. The details and procedures are vastly different from the stories that have come down to us via that bible I mentioned elsewhere.

Since most of the stories of the bible are from just one small portion of our planet, they concern only the tribes of that region—primarily the tribes of Northern Africa and the Mediterranean region that inherited the broken pieces of the progression of empires that came before what has been called the Christian Era. While the church sought to discredit the vast body of knowledge of those before it, it had no other model with which to govern. As a result, the church borrowed rather liberally from the religious practices of Kempt, Greece and Rome.

Over the centuries, the tribes of white humans were given the impression that the planet was for them to take and they did just that. A major part of this story line was the fact that man had fallen from grace. Over the centuries, this narrative has become gospel in the eyes of some of us on the planet, but not all.

There are many in our nation of today who are convinced that we are truly living in the 'end times'. There are to be, of course, survivors of this event.

***All human fables about great
planetary upheavals have survivors.***

It's very easy to get caught up in this present religious frenzy. Human events of the day give many reason to quote past prophets and their dire predictions about the fate of man. What most don't realize is that these prophets had their focus on the corrupt empires of Europe and their use of warfare to gain access to land and mineral wealth. To them then, and to a lot of their descendants in America today, the only human that matter are those of the white tribes of Europe.

All predictions and prophecies, like religion itself, are a matter of interpretation. Those who want their view to become that of others will use these predictions to their own end.

What many in America don't know is that in the brief history of our white brother, these predictions of doom and destruction are cyclical—showing up at the end of each century. At the end of ten centuries, the predictions become tenfold. In the world of today with almost instant communication on a planetary scale, it's very difficult **NOT** to hear this story line over and over, from all its varied interpreters.

What I find interesting about my white brother's version of this upcoming event is the actions that are to be taken by the demigod (the offspring of that supreme being and the mortal female). According to many interpretations of this upcoming event, this individual is to return to our planet and 'set things straight'.

Therein lies the rub.

Just whose standard is going to be used in this 'setting things straight.'? The impression I get from the various interpretations is that all those who do not fit this 'standard' will be swept away, eliminated, reduced to molecular dust, cast into the depths of hell, vaporized, etc., etc., etc.

The concept or idea of hell is another part of my white brother's tribal story that is relatively new. In actuality it's his version of the underworld of the ancient world with changes. In the world prior to the arrival of the christian era, the underworld, in many cultures, was a testing area for man. Resisting temptation, testing one's faith, overcoming adversity—these were the tests that man had to endure in the underworld when he found himself there. It was a place to grow spiritually, mentally and emotionally.

In the creation story of the Mayans, twin boys endured and survived tests thrown at them by the lords of the underworld. When the twins emerged from that region, the world and the cosmos were created for them. They had passed the tests and were rewarded with the planet and all that was in the heavens.

In the creation story from the fertile crescent that survives in the bible, there is only one central character and the focus has been shifted to that one individual. His adventure into what used to be the 'underworld' and his 'triumph' over death is the reason for his adoration by those who accept these stories as fact. After his resurrection and subsequent departure from earth, it is reported that he would return someday. This 'returning' of a god or the gods is quite common to many human fables. The citizens of the one of the empires of Central America thought the Spanish conquistadors were returning gods. They even thought the men on horseback was one creature.

In the case of the Christian myths, will this returning demigod be that desired by the Ku Klux Klan who want him to get rid of all black humans and those humans that follow the religion of Israel? Or will all the abortionists and gay people be done away with to suit the purposes of the bigoted religious right of adolescent America? Better yet, since these fables go beyond the borders of the religion that America supports, what about the infidels who have heaped abuse upon those who follow Islam? Will this returning entity "set things straight" by wiping out all those who don't support the teachings of Mohammed? Since this adolescent nation has so many who complain about how 'bad' the world is, he or she is going to be rather busy meeting the demands of all these different interpretations of how the planet should be operated.

We have even been told of the birth of an "anti-Christ" or alter ego to this demigod. The idea is that this individual is the product of a union between Satan, the alter ego and opposite of the supreme being and, you guessed it, a mortal female. I seem to also recall a concept called a 'false peace' that comes out in this narrative. After the end of this 'false peace', the final conflict (Armageddon) between the supreme beings (light and dark) is to take place, with Earth being the battle ground.

At this point, I would like to ask the reader a question.

What's so special about this planet???

If, as we have been told, that this supreme being created all of what we can now see—*the vast and seemingly limitless distances of space*—it would seem to me that he or she is still creating all that we call the universe and really wouldn't be interested in what happens here. We now know that many other planetary bodies like ours exist in all of this marvelous cosmos. The idea that the creator has some special affinity for this one planet springs from the mind of an ignorant and arrogant puppy who knows how to do nothing other than steal.

Granted, my white brother is clever, but he really hasn't been very intelligent, particularly since his brain was wiped clean by the church and spoon fed his particular brand of rudeness and arrogance that has irritated many of us who share this planet with him.

One of the societies that lived on the plains of this continent prior to the arrival of my white brother tells of a creator that is to return to take them to another planet wherein they can continue caring for that place as was their job here. Using the planet for profit was unknown to them.

Cousins of these humans to the south tell of the end of a 'long count'. At the end of that cycle, "time, as we know it, shall cease to exist". This intriguing statement sends the mind in a different direction altogether than the fables handed down to us from the Semitic tribes. These humans also tell us that our spiritual growth and maturation is tied to the life of the planet. As it changes, so shall we.

We're just about due for another one of those planetary flip flops. One member of the family, with the name of Immanuel, has told us that our home has actually become unstable and flipped on its axis several times in its very long her-story. As the continents move about, the weights shift and the planet wobbles until it restores itself to a state of balance.

I find this line of thinking much more plausible and fascinating than another tired tale about another war. We've all had enough war, both the human variety and the non-human variety.

Keep your eyes on our planet, It will soon give you enough new data to clear your mind of all those desert myths.

The Dictator Gene

Our knowledge of the forms in which we all live increases day by day. We now know that the genetic code is responsible for the shape, color, longevity, operation and overall state of these bodies.

Other human factors such as personality traits are now suspected to be influenced by genetics as well. For many decades, the debate over nature and nurture has raged within the halls of academia over this very topic.

I'm of the opinion that within the male of our species, a gene exists that channels the power and talents of an individual into the role we identify as dictatorial. Since we're talking about his-story, a brief look at the late, great *successful* war celebrated by our nation continually might illustrate this phenomenon.

We usually refer to Adolf Hitler in this sense, but the pattern manifested itself on our planet in more places that Germany. The bad guys dictators, in addition to Adolf, were Benito Mussolini in Italy and Tojo in Japan. A bad guy who started out a good guy was Josef Stalin. In my opinion, of all the dictators that appeared in our species during this time, the Russians got the most virulent example.

On the so-called good guy side, there were several benign and virulent examples as well. Ronald Reagan had his own reasons for calling FDR a dictator, but he was one of the benign versions, as was Churchill in England. Franco of Spain was benign, with some slights traits of virulence, and France got Charles DeGaulle, primarily benign with his virulence being confined to his earlier military life, but a dictator all the same.

On the American scene, we denied and continue to deny the dictatorial traits of J. Edgar Hoover. The white boys who controlled Congress stood by like frightened fools while Joseph McCarthy shit all over the Constitution. It was only after McCarthy attacked the military that Congress took any action against this virulent expression of the dictator gene. Their reluctance to do anything against that senator from Wisconsin only underscores the tendency of some white males to deny reality a lot.

The United States made overall planetary conditions much worse by supporting a succession of dictators anywhere they could be found. Although he was championed as a fighter for democracy, the creator of Time magazine failed to call Chiang Kai Shek a dictator. Madame Chiang had some of these tendencies as well, but this phenomenon appears to be primarily male. All the leaders of the nations in our hemisphere that various Republican and Democratic administrations supported were dictators. The Somozas in Nicaragua, the Bautistas in Cuba, the duValliers in Haiti, and Pinochet in Argentina—all were dictators. In other parts of the world, the US supported dictators such as Ferdinand Marcos in the Philippines, Idi Amin Dada in Africa, and Hallie Sellasie in Ethiopia.

At the behest of the oil cartel, the Shah of Iran was put in place after the duly elected president was discredited with the help of the US. Reza Pahlavi even went so far as to trace his roots back to another dictator in the very long history of Persia. He claimed to be descended from Darius.

As Judy Tanuda would say, "It could happen".

The so-called royal family of Saudi Arabia is a dictatorship that was set up by the Seven Sisters early on in the 20th century. Saddam Hussein is only reacting, albeit in a typically male dictatorial fashion, to the actions of neighboring dictators. Haffas Ashad recently left us and nobody understands what mental processes drove the dictators in Afghanistan.

Governments built around theology are dictatorships with self-blessings from the ones in office at the time.

Marshall Tito, in retrospect, turned out to be not so bad after all. After that winter Olympic party and his death, Yugoslavia imploded and we all got Milosevich. Sorry about that, sports fans.

Chairman Mao, a Chinese version of this gene, did have perspective, however. It was he, in response to the question as to whether the French Revolution was a success, who said, "Too soon to tell." The dictators who followed him, the Chinese named most aptly—"The Gang of Four". Again, this gene is not limited to males, but this is where it shows up most frequently. As more females become leaders, we may see the trait demonstrated in them as well. Indira Ghandi used some of those techniques and paid with her life.

The Romanians finally put an end to the lives of Nicolas Ceausescu and his wife. They got fed up with them after that couple took all the silver out of Elizabeth's guesthouse in London following a state visit. Just too tacky!

When the people of Liberia got fed up with the Tubmans, they took them out to the beach and shot them. Now there's an idea.

The Roman senate was all prepared to offer Julius Caesar the position of Dictator for Life, but killed him when they feared that he would make himself king or emperor, something they disliked immensely. Those personal daggers do come in handy sometimes.

Despite his elevation to the status of superstar by western educators, Alexander the Great was a dictator, as was his father, Phillip. Those same academics had no such problems with the term describing the Mongol versions, those Khan guys, Genghis and his grandson, Kublia, who was actually another benign example.

Vlad, the Impaler, did his dictatorial thing for the Catholic Church until they finally turned him off. Digging those holes in the ground with stakes and all; he definitely went overboard just a bit.

That's also where that vampire myth originated.

Ludwig, the Mad Bavarian, played the dictator until he was finally snuffed out. He and his doctor just disappeared after going for a walk by the lake one day. Nobody wanted to be broke and he was using up all the money. Besides, he had this thing about young men that was not in vogue in those days, even for a mad dictator.

So the next time you read the New York Times, Washington Post. LA Times or some other national rag waxing eloquently about this or that dictator, remember, it's another one of those male things.

Comes with the species.

Leave That Boy Alone!!!

He's only done what we taught him. He learned his lesson well. He and those other guys on the other side of town started out pretty much with the same idea, that went in different directions for a number of reasons.

Different humans, different realities.

In typical fashion, when the idea of the computer began to grow, older males with money were essentially tied to the pattern set by the colonial ethic and thinking. If it's not big, it's not of any value. If we see no immediate potential in something to fit the next quarter's projections, then it's not worth investigating.

Like all original operating systems for any computer, both the PC and the MAC had their original instructions and commands given to them via the keyboard. As the commands grew more and more complex and lengthy, an easier method had to be devised that would give the computer these increasingly complex commands. The idea that the individual citizen did indeed have the knowledge to operate these computer things was starting to catch on. The written word is fine, but as the old adage goes, a picture is worth a thousand words. Besides, we're all living in a time that was vastly influenced by selective editing of the written word.

So the need for a visual input device became apparent with this new thing called a computer. However, those young guys at a company named after a fruit were having a mental block at the time and the next part of their puzzle showed up on their doorstep from outside their sphere, courtesy of some other guys from another side of town.

That mouse thing came from, oddly enough, a big company. This big company happened to have a small division of their corporation in the same town where the two Steves and Bill lived. However, those in command of the big company saw no value in this new device and let it languish on the creative branch, so to speak.

Just to see their idea put to use, the guys who actually thought up the mouse, decided to contact some younger guys on the other side of town who might see value in their idea. So the two Steves got a phone call from some frustrated inventors.

Recognizing the potential in this thing with a tail, they jumped at the offer. The first full use of this new input device showed up with the Mac. It had been out there in rudimentary form but this new shape stuck.

Besides, this particular rodent and my
white brother have a long association.
It's a mammal that shows up
in his literature most frequently.

A lot of us liked the approach of the two Steves. Their idea was to give the customer a complete system out the door. Since the other young guy on the other side of town was into software big time, he didn't focus his direction on hardware. The two Steves were different and decided to produce the entire product, software **and** hardware, under the same roof.

Different people, different realities.

So Bill has only come out with a few hardware items, one being that keyboard, which by the way, was a good idea. It recognized the fact that none of us sits up and hold our hands and arms the way we were taught in typing class.

Concentrating on both hardware and software had its disadvantages from the standpoint of wanting to be the biggest. In that respect, Bill outdid his contemporaries on the other side of town.

His flair for the market forces enabled this young member of our species to amass great wealth relatively quickly. As Sam Walton was preparing to leave us, Bill was gaining more and more capital. He recognized that the key to this was in the software and worked out arrangements with all the producers of hardware, anywhere on the planet, to put his operating system in their machines as they went out the door.

The production of and innovation to hardware occurs at a faster rate and has a quicker return on the investment. That part of the market grew like a dandelion. Software production lags behind. However, as ideas change, so does the software. Everything of a hardware nature showing up in the computer has been here a long time. It's the software that's really new. Besides, Bill's been making money and the market just loves a money maker. Grow and grow. So much so, that before anyone realized it, Bill and his buddies were controlling the direction of a major portion of both the software and hardware markets.

Great wealth creates enemies and detractors. Besides, the human male can be a very vindictive person. When I was a child I learned that pettiness, vindictiveness, bitchiness and other such character traits were the purview of the female. I eventually discovered that I had been grossly misinformed.

Some older males became extremely jealous of this boy—how dare he make all that money, and so early in his life. That's not supposed to happen. He hasn't bothered to come to Washington at all, so he's got to be doing something wrong. Let's accuse him of monopolistic practices. That should take the wind out of his sails.

I should go get my hip boots. It's getting pretty deep in here.

This boy has been watching the likes of Warren Buffett, Sam Walton, General Motors, the not-so-fabulous Hunt Brothers, the oil companies, the energy companies and good old GE. He and the rest of us were watching when we starting play monopoly, big time, in the late 70s. We all watched the growth of the "multinationals" and heard ADM brag about being "supermarket to the world". We've seen the frenzy of buying, merging and selling that has not abated. The rapid consolidation of the media industry is probably the best example of all. These human enterprises are monopolies, if not by design, then by intent. This is another example of do what I say, not what I do. This amazing duplicity is the hallmark of the Protestant ethic. It's the forked tongue syndrome.

You greedy guys leave that boy alone.

Don't Bring Me No Bad News

That McVeigh boy has brought white American bad news, big time.

They really weren't ready for one of their own children, bright and intelligent, telling them about themselves and the example they've been setting across our marvelous planet.

This white child grew up and followed the possibilities offered him by the culture. Being a male, he followed the male thing to be a soldier. Evidently he did well in his chosen profession and learned his lessons.

That phrase we heard during the reports of the event, 'collateral damage', is Pentagon-ese, the jargon of the military industrial complex. We heard the debate about this term and its apparent callousness. If it is a callous disregard for life, then its something he learned it at the foot of America.

Denial, BIG TIME.

"Acceptable losses" is another one of these terms. We were reminded of this in the popular media in one of Bruce Willis's movies—the one about the robbery by the usual German bad guys. Their plan was to rob a financial center of its stocks and bonds. The government types, coming in to save the day, were willing to sacrifice a certain percentage of the hostages in order to catch the culprits. "I can live with that" was the comment made. Ask the guys who came back from Vietnam with their minds relatively unscathed and they'll tell you about a whole bunch of such terms.

This white boy was only doing what we taught him.

If anyone cares to hear, this boy is telling white America that it is not setting such a good example as a society to the rest of the human family. For his own reasons, he focused in on what happened to other "white" dissenters, malcontents, as it were, and the way in which the power structure responded to these outbreaks.

Us black folk have been talking about this for some time now, but since white America has never really paid much attention to anything we say, our words have fallen upon ears that have been deaf to us for centuries.

> ***You can cook my food, cut my lawn,***
> ***clean my home, drive my car,***
> ***watch after my kids,***
> ***but don't have an opinion.***

So, imagine my surprise and delight when I discovered that it was a white boy that was behind this latest demonstration of the inherent violence of our species, honed by hundreds of years of religious carnage.

Predictably, at the time, some other white boy with access to the media and its influence announced that it was an Arab terrorist who destroyed that federal building and killed all those humans. Those Arab guys get blamed for a lot of stuff that America does.

What's that all about?

This boy was only doing what we taught him.

Us black folk are used to being killed by whites, in so many ways, it defies the imagination. Seeing more of our kind killed in this very ungrateful and indifferent system was nothing new to us. Naturally, white folks would want to blame someone other than themselves when it happens to them. Pointing the finger somewhere else didn't work this time.

BATMAN SOUNDS RIGHT IN THE SOLAR PLEXUS.

So, they've reached back into their tribal memory and pulled up an old practice of killing the delivery person bringing the news.

Don't you dare bring me no bad news!

Cottonballs

I had a little idea,
but it flitted right out of my mind and went into an idea-holding pen,
joining other thoughts of its kind—

to be thought by someone else,
when his brain's in the receiving mode, for ideas are free
and belong to a universal code.

The thing to remember is to leave your mind's switch on open,
never on close;
for if it's in the latter position,
you might as well stuff cottonballs up your nose.

Venice
1979

The Gunpowder Blues

I'm sure there are some Chinese citizens who are re-thinking their act of kindness that gave the white boy that knowledge about gunpowder back in the 14th century. While Europe was in an intellectual basement, the Chinese were building walls that can be seen from off the planet. They were, like the rest of us, having the usual tribal warfare conflicts. They were developing that porcelain that had never been seen before in Europe, coming up with the concept of paper money, devising the noodle (made with rice flour, however), trading with East Africa and India, living by and with the tenets of Confuscious, keeping their turmoil pretty much at home, and doing other neat stuff.

These white boys from the emerging nations of the old Roman Empire showed up one day at their door. Being the gracious hosts that the human family is noted for, the Chinese extended the welcome mat to these hardy travelers and proceeded to show them around the house.

"Make yourself at home, have some green tea and rice cakes; try these noodles with soy sauce and we'll talk of things interesting."

Meanwhile, back in Europe, the lights of knowledge had been off for some time. Those hardy travelers had heard that there was all sorts of action far away and had come to check it out. Slowly, but surely, the flames of the intellectual light were beginning to flicker, ever so faintly, in their homeland.

So after each visit, these white explorers came back to their homes with tales of wonders and a few gifts from this strange and marvelous land filled with the people that were not white, but light in complexion with different shaped eyes. They also had this stuff they called silk they wore all over the place. It seemed a miracle at the time.

On one of these return trips, one of these travelers brought back a particular mixture of chemicals that was called black powder. The Chinese, for the most part, used this chemical knowledge in the celebration of life and to act as a deterrent against evil spirits they believed lived here with us. Although a few grenades and other implements of war were made in China during this time, (an almost logical extension of this technology), the Chinese, for the most part, used this physical knowledge in a non-combative fashion. They still do to this very day, primarily. It's only after recent contact with my white brother that they've turned their considerable talents to weapons of mass destruction.

Such was not the case with the white boys.

Once that knowledge began to spread among the tribes of Europe, they set about almost immediately making devices that could do in their nearest tribal enemy—blow him to bits.

The cannon soon evolved into an effective device to blow the walls of a competing tribe's city to smithereens. Along with this cannon came the knowledge of trajectories (rediscovered math), metallurgy, city planning and naval warfare. Bigger ships were built to carry bigger guns, and the empire race was on. The trials and tribulations of the African continent was to soon begin. In our time it has finally ended.

When the first white tribes found out how to sail to the east by going around the tip of Africa, they stopped along the way for food and provisions. They ran into all those black people on the eastern side of that vast continent. They, too, made these new visitors welcome in their land. Upon their initial visit, the Portuguese, who were the first to do this traveling bit out of dark age Europe, found these black people wearing all this gold—rings, necklaces, anklets—gold used in all manner of decoration. It was decorating their buildings and such. It was a status symbol in these cultures, not something associated with wealth. Wealth was measured in other things.

Different people, different realities.

Something else they discovered on their first venture into this part of the planet—these black people, for the most part, were unChristian. They were Moslems.

Well, this situation was definitely intolerable. These Moslem people are infidels, non-believers that are doomed to be cast into the pits of hell. They worship Mohammed, who didn't believe in Jesus. So, they can't allowed to be here. We must convert them to our way of thinking or kill them in the process.

Two years after the first visit to Eastern Africa the boys from Portugal came back, this time, with gunboats.

By the time the white boys of Europe began to break the mind lock the Catholic Church had on them, they believed that the planet was theirs for the taking. Since they were convinced they possessed the only true faith, everyone else was a non-believer and had to be converted, even killed, in order to save their souls.

The reality of this story is that the Catholic Church was desperately trying to rebuild the old Roman Empire, the only example of government and method of running things that was on their tribal horizon at the time. Consequently, any different religious thought, method of running a society and organization that human activity requires, was suspect if they had not seen it before.

The total effect of this attitude is that wherever the white boy showed up with his bible and his guns, those members of the species that had been living in those places went immediately into slavery. They didn't get a chance to pass Go, collect $200 or get a Get-Out-of-Jail-Free card.

Once the Christianized and gun-powdered tribes of Europe found out about the continents of Africa, the Americas and the rest of the planet, they set about christianizing it and depriving the locals of their mineral wealth and the best land in the land. There are few exceptions to this rule. China, India and Japan and parts of the world where other methods of thought still abide were able to deflect the forces of the white tribes. In these areas, this imported religious ethic did not stick.

As time went along, some of these white boys played around with this black powder stuff the Chinese had given them and made it even stronger. Alfred Nobel did this the best and made lots of money with his version of the black powder that he called dynamite. Later on, expanding on this concept, the logical extension of this mentality was the evolution of the atomic bomb, since we needed to make bigger and better bombs to blow up bigger and better things.

This white boy got his hands on that black powder and has been blowing up shit ever since.

Another white boy just blew up a building in a state called Oklahoma. I think that name is a word from the language of one of the original societies that inhabited this continent before the arrival of you-know-who. Seems like that gunpowder evolved into something else and came back and bit my white brother on his butt.

He's got the gunpowder blues.

You Go Girl!!

The Original Cross-Dresser—

was a female
had a male lover but didn't marry him
wore a beard like a male
ran city hall
figured out a way to slow down the thieves
built a passal of monuments (it was all the rage in those days)
got discredited after her death
made it possible for us to find King Tut's burial site
built herself a fabulous tomb not too far from that of her lover,
together forever
for us in our time, had a most difficult name to pronounce, Hatshet-
sup, shortened immediately to Hat

It was her idea, I've been told, to go out there in that valley to continue
that tomb construction flair those folks had; seems that pyramid building thing had turned out to be not such a good idea after all; when you
build such things, they **do** get noticed.

Robbing graves has been a human thing for a long time.
Early American doctors had to resort to robbing graves
in order to have cadavers upon which to study their craft.
Doctors weren't trusted in those days, you know.

So, to slow down the thieves and insure that she and those who followed her would not be forgotten, the tombs of Egypt were built underground from a certain point in time forward.

Cleopatra played Rome and its two famous males for all they were worth and then left us in grand style when she saw that the end of her beloved Egypt was at hand.

In the world of the Carthegenians, a competing and equal black society that was a contemporary of Rome, Dido was a famous queen whose beauty and intellect was known far and wide. She also sent troops into war.

The so-called "cradle of democracy" didn't allow its females to vote.

So much for democracy.

The women of Switzerland just got the vote in the latter half of the 20th century. That's bloody recent, if you ask me.

When females are rulers,
it may be a logical decision
NOT to get married to their male lovers.

Elizabeth the First did the same thing as Queen Hat. She, too, recognized that if she married "her man", the rest of the males in her system would ignore her and gravitate to the male, and do the male thing.

Then she proceeded to alter her complexion.

It seemed to have worked. The British Empire could not have become the system it did had she not done "her thing". Even her cousin, Mary, who got trapped in that Catholic/Protestant debacle, had potential that never came to fruition. She eventually lost her head over the whole affair.

Catherine the Great, the "mother of all the Russias" didn't get caught in that marriage thing either, at least not actually. She even had a brief affair with one of our naval heroes, a guy named Jones. He went over to Russia out of frustration when the Congress of that time proved to be too cheap and refused to pay him for his past services and unwanted advice.

Sound familiar???

George Sand, whose real name was Amandine Lucile Dupin, took the name of a male so she could have her written works published. Writers have always used the "nom-de-plume" and she profited from this cultural habit. It seems that Catholic France wasn't so keen to hear from a female writer. They had been taught that females did not possess such talents. She apparently had enough talent to be called "the greatest writer of our time" by many of her day.

Over here in the new country, males who were to become icons in the nation's his-story were becoming so because many of them married well. These male icons were usually broke or poor, so the women in their lives provided the capital that drove their careers, fame and, ultimately, their places in his-story.

Lili'uokalani, the last queen of Hawaii, who was also an accomplished song writer, came to Washington to speak to Congress. While riding the train from the West Coast to DC, she saw the vastness of the white man's world and wondered why they were scheming to take her 'little islands' when they had all of this. She called them 'rude people' and had to watch her nation become overrun by these 'white locusts'.

The northern planetary white tribes, typically small societies by design and geography, have had numerous female rulers, and much to their credit, have had fairly consistent operation of their systems over all.

The Dutch, in particular, had a succession of female monarchs and seemed to have evolved a rather perceptive society, a concept our adolescent nation is just beginning to realize even exists. Then again, the Dutch did recognize early on that their lives and well being are decided by the planet. The Zeider Zee was a force to be respected.

In Andalusia, now called Spain, Isabella survived several attempts on her life, orchestrated by her own brother no less, to become the Catholic icon and darling of Rome. Speaking of the Spain and the Catholic Church, we can't forget about that Borgia lady, Lucrezia. Whether or not her reputation is accurate or deserved, it only indicates that women can be just as ruthless as men, given the opportunity.

Cory Aquino stepped in to redirect her country after the males did the usual assassination thing to her husband. Males can be so typical at times.

I've already mentioned Indira Ghandi and the response her actions elicited from the males in her system.

In early 20th century America, the first female to become a millionaire was Madame C. J. Walker. She made her money manufacturing hair care products for black citizens.

Lizzie Borden was ultimately acquitted of doing her parents in because the males of the time were incapable of accepting the fact that the female is capable of murder as well as the male, albeit on a much smaller scale.

In their minds I suppose females
were only good at listening to serpents.

In typical fashion some males from a nearby immigrant community were the first to be arrested for those ax murders up in Fallbrook, Massachusetts. We now know that Lizzie done the dirty deed.

FDR did have some good ideas that benefited the rest of the country and black folks benefited as well. However, the Roosevelt black people **actually** like is Eleanor, his wife. She really did fly in that plane with that black pilot, whom the white males said didn't have the intelligence to do so. She also told the snobbish DAR she no longer wanted to be a member of that ignorant organization. She then proceeded to make it possible for Marian Anderson to sooth us all with her lush contralto. Turns out, the crowd that showed up at the Lincoln Memorial that clear and chilly day wouldn't have fit in the tired Constitution Hall anyway. Before she left us, the Lady from Philadelphia also broke the color line at the then stodgy Metropolitan Opera.

Wilma Rudolph overcame the ravages of polio to win Olympic Gold by dazzling us all with her speed. She had survived the panic and hysteria that followed the arrival of that particular virus. FDR chose to hide his paralysis.

The male-dominated media empire in this place can't find enough dirt to throw at Senator Hillary Clinton, so they keep digging around and 'finding' new facts to publish. If she does run for president, then watch how much new dirt we will suddenly 'discover'.

Senator Clinton's ex-counterpart in England, Cherie Booth, another accomplished lawyer and the wife of the prime minister, is the darling of the beer industry over there. She has been most successful in their fight to gain parity on the world market. Then again, the British have had a much longer relationship with female rulers and thinkers.

Hollywood will be forever grateful to Mary Shelley for Frankenstein.

Besides, the English have had some males that were real airheads as kings and would-be-kings. In our own time, it has also been said that Margaret Thatcher, their first female prime minister, was really Ronald Reagan in drag.

Ask any USNaval or computer historian about Capt. Allen and her contribution to the world of computers.

Lana Turner proved that beauty and brains can go hand in hand when she invented a key portion of the bombardier's gun sight used in the bombers of the second great white tribal war. Another great beauty, Ingrid Bergman, originated the idea of digital wireless communication.

We won't even begin to mention the impact the ladies have had on the various entertainment industry sections and the world of sports. Even today, they're still not getting their 'propers'.

So the next time you hear a debate about this young place electing a female as president, think on these family facts I've presented to you here.

All I have to say in response is, "You Go Girl".

From a Time in His-story

—comes the story of human babies being delivered by a large migratory bird-one of the stork family-birds with great wingspans. It seems that this particular planetary resident took to building its nest on the chimneys of the homes in which the tribes of Europe lived. The birds would show up around springtime as the weather grew warmer. Since the human beings of the area had been entombed in their homes for the winter, the usual result several months later would be a new addition to the family. Since no one could read and knowledge about reproduction was no longer in their minds, the association with the bird became accepted.

Of course, your next question would be, why didn't these people know about babies and the act of reproduction? They had dogs and other animals. Rats were everywhere, literally. They must have noticed the similarity in how these neighbors came to be and how we came to be in these forms.

In our time we still sometimes see images of babies and birds. The birds may be different, but the concept is the same.

Those of you with very young children get ready for the questions about where babies come from. It is encouraging to see mothers nursing their babies with the organs provided by these forms.

To find myself living in a society
that has found this act repulsive
seems acutely bizarre and demented.

So this fear and loathing of things sexual and the process of birth had its start somewhere in his-story.

In our time the birthing process has been designed for the benefit of the priests of the medical profession, originally set up by males. Those stirrups that women have to use when delivering were devised for the convenience of the doctor. It's much more natural for the birthing process to take place using the forces of gravity. Better yet, the process is best performed under water. Ask those females who have given birth under water. They'll tell you.

I remember the vicious letters written to Life magazine when we discovered photography using fiber optics and the development of the human fetus was first seen outside the confines of the womb. The level of ignorance and fear of "how we get here" is slowly decreasing. However, much of it is still present.

Farmers and their families have a better understanding of the birthing process and are probably in a much better position to appreciate the same process in our own species. However, much of what we are told today comes from those small-minded individuals who use ignorance and fear to line their own pockets with "fear money".

Much of my white brother's history is couched in terms of the level of fear generated by the mind-control he lived under for so many centuries.

Fear of the dark is another thing that seems to have been exaggerated in these tribal members. Africans, the original Australians, the original Americans, and most other tribal members of our species understood the night world and used it to their advantage. It was only after the brainwashing of the church that our paleface brother developed this unhealthy fear of things in the dark.

The poor bat is one immediate example that comes to mind of a creature who has suffered because of the abysmal ignorance about creatures that are nocturnal, who operate while we're asleep. If it weren't for this particular flying mammal with that echo-locating thing in their brains (radar), the banana plant would not be pollinated and we couldn't have bananas on our cereals in the morning. It was the fear of the night that was successful in putting the cat in a bad light in early Europe. Besides, by the time the devil had been created by the church (after Dante had published his famous poem), all things dark became evil, including some members of the same human family.

Why do they call them 'deviled eggs'?

You Can't Dance In Here

In his age of exploration, my white brother attacked the rituals and dancing of all he met, especially if it was perceived to be too overtly sexual.

As reported by a history professor from the University of Hawaii: "When the white missionaries first came to our land, they stopped us from dancing. These were people from New England, who didn't like *any* kind of dancing. They didn't even celebrate Christmas, something most other groups calling themselves Christian did."

The ritual of dancing is an important part of the human makeup. It is something that all of us do, no matter what kind of music is played. Only a mind that was locked away in darkness could ever reach such a state of un-awareness.

Even the waltz and the polka were subjects of disdain at one time in my white brother's his-tory. They were seen as too radical and unconventional by the power structure of the day. They were perceived as threats to the order of the day.

Those of us whose blood lines arose in Africa experienced the suppression of our dances and rituals as well. As a result of this suppression, that energy took form in the confines of the black church in America. When the rituals of the religion practiced by the tribes of Europe became the law of the land, all other forms of worship went underground. Since the slave was left alone to his own devices when he wasn't doing "his job", the ex-patriated Africans continued to sing and dance in his own churches.

Even poor whites suffered at the hands of the elite of their own tribe. The religions of power and wealth looked down their noses at the religious practices of the poor whites of Appalachia and made fun of them in the popular media for years. Only recently, as our adolescent nation has begun to inch forward to its true identity has this ridicule of their own kind ceased.

The United States Army committed one of the greatest of their many atrocities against the plains Indians when they massacred those members of the community that practiced the last "ghost dance". To those original Americans, that particular dance was used to call upon the power of their ancestors for assistance. The whites of the day were so totally ignorant about these people, that they actually feared the power of the "dance" and sought to stamp it out by killing them.

Could this have been a tribal memory
that haunted them from their own ancient past,
raising doubts about their present state of mind?

When the 'King' started gyrating his hips on American television, white America was incensed that its children were attracted to this white version of "race music". It was too sexually suggestive. On the television, the cameramen were instructed not to photograph Elvis below the belt. However, the teenagers had money and money was being made by all who wanted more, so rock and roll did not die, as many experts of the day had predicted. Lots of established white stars recognized the value in this "newly acquired art form" and started copying black music for profit.

So much for expert opinions.

In the seventies, the music called disco was literally driven away from the country by those white males who saw it as threatening to their realties because it was too "gay" oriented. Consequently, it went to other parts of the world where it flourished, evolved and returned as techno-pop. Even the masterful George Clinton [no relation to Bill (at least I don't think so)] helped to bring it back to these shores in its new form. Now all our children, no matter what color, are dancing to this new form of an old music.

Who say's you can't dance in here?

To the Mahalia Imitators

This whole thing you seek to save may not be the way it was supposed
to be
What you think is real and what is not may not be what you think you
see
You seem not to understand the presence of a being in a form like
mine and me
Sounds like you been listening the rude strains of the sirens of Christianity.

That man they're always talkin' about didn't say a thing at all 'bout me
Com' to think, I don't remember him saying anything at all about
thee.
I don't think that trap is really where he wanted you and your brain to
be
In the job of repairing the damage what's been done us all by Christianity.

Look outside the land of us and the things you think you want to be
Look into the near and distant past to find your part in this thing
called history.
The answers are dancing here but you don't really know what you can
see—
Brain static caused by thoughts planted there by this man's Christianity.

There are other and older minds on this planet that is home to you and
me
Go search them out beneath the newly inflicted rubble that you should
see
That what you've been told is not the way it is or was supposed to be
That's one of the tricks played on you by those guys from Christianity.

What's so sad about the things you've said in response to my enjoying
me
Is that you think that you have to fear the presence of someone unlike
thee
So that you can have things in the way you've been told they're supposed to be
Reciting the company line from the guys dressed in white from Christianity.

Your talents are best directed against the madness within your own sex-
uality
Casting dispersions at me can not give you enough plausible deniabil-
ity
You've been deceived by those overtaxed by their own gnawing insecu-
rity
Leading empty and desperate lives to impress you with their style of
Christianity.

My being is an expression of this planet's life in all its maddening
diversity
But then again, it seems you're either not willing or unable to begin to
see
That my manifestation since the beginning was part of what was sup-
posed to be
Things left out of that book with the missing pages handed out by
Christianity.

You are children of wealth and power and that carries with it responsi-
bility
Get your facts correct before you display the thoughts of your minds
for all to see
Or you may get more letters from parts of the planetary family who
agree with me
That your thinkin's showing the effects of the royal scam calling itself
Christianity.

Please Signal Before Changing Lanes!

Somewhere I read that it was the Romans who first started building things with concrete. While they and everyone else had been using marble, granite, sandstone and the various building materials supplied by their local area, those Roman guys needed something for their ever-expanding empire that would establish their culture wherever they set up shop. Granted, being the practical guys they were, they utilized local materials wherever they went as well. However, it was after adding that limestone portion to a slurry of ground stone that gave them the concrete formula that we all know and love today. However, the mixture of today is vastly different from that used a couple of thousand years ago and cannot stand the test of time that their original formula has.

Different people, different realities.

What we use today is designed to be constructed quickly. Our mechanized culture is evolving at such a dizzying pace, it's all we can do to keep up with the changes associated just with the automobile.

Those Germans guys are generally credited with creating the concept of the freeway. Being the efficient and practical-minded folks they are, they figured out that the car could serve its best purpose if it was unrestricted and provided with a closed system for travel within their homeland. Like the rest of us, they had to learn about the "problems" of this approach as time went along. However, at the time it sounded like a good idea, and in some ways, it still is.

Over here in the colonies, however, we had our own way of doing things. Besides, this place is a much larger piece of real estate than the area known as Germany. In addition, we hadn't had our manufacturing base destroyed in tribal wars as had Germany, so we continued with this imported idea unfettered by a slow-down in the industrial sector of the society.

So, when Dwight David proposed the idea of a system of roads to provide a fast exit from cities that had just been "nuked", the concrete boys saw gigantic dollar signs and jumped on the band wagon with both feet. The congress of the day had swallowed the insane fears of that paranoid alcoholic senator from Wisconsin and funded the building of the rudimentary freeway system that has evolved to what we have today.

Since evolution is a dirty word in Protestant America, it is essential that every present-day citizen visit the City of the Angeles to understand that evolution is what it's all about, particularly regarding the American version of that German idea.

You guys who live in the East Coast cities have toll roads, turnpikes, expressways, beltways, highways, etc. The term freeway probably originated in the Golden State because there were no collection booths on them. That's a relatively unused idea in that state and, even today, there are very few toll roads so familiar to those citizens in most other states.

El Pueblo de la Reina de Nuestra Senora de Los Angeles is our planet's best expression of the use and misuse of the automobile. One must journey to see, first hand, how that old Roman idea and the new colonial motoring idea have been married to produce this ever evolving city. Eventually San Diego, the largest city to the south and LA will be one continuous city. It is, for all intent and purposes, that way today. Presently, the only impediment to that happening, in fact, is the military machine. As our system matures, we shall eventually learn that war making is not an intelligent method of performance any society. With that realization, that military obstacle between San Diego and LA will be removed and our species will see the first example of how we will live on other planets.

Despite the built in inefficiencies, LA and San Diego work.

The destruction of the idea of mass transit was necessary in order for LA to develop to its present state. Mass transit is a collective or communistic concept. It is no accident that the destruction of the local train systems across the nation began during the reign of that alcoholic senator I mentioned elsewhere. Once that collective concept was laid to rest, the individual transportation unit became the norm and the roads to use them was the next logical step on our way to where we are now.

For those of you who don't live in LA or San Diego, the pictures of the freeways of Southern Cali that you get in the movies are rather limited. An old TV show called "CHiP's" would probably be the best example of what the freeway system looked like, and by today's standards, it's outdated, like most of the movies Hollywood does that use the freeways as a backdrop. Besides, most of what we usually see involving freeway car chases take place in the Los Angeles river basin. It's built of concrete also and is usually dry during most of the year. The Hollywood machine doesn't have enough money to stop the traffic on real freeways to shoot silly drug and/or robbery chase movies.

Many road scenes of "CHiP's" were filmed on the 210 freeway. The 210 is part of the Interstate system and was built to connect Interstate 405 with Interstate 10.

Interstate 10 is named after, of all people,
Christopher Columbus. It starts in Santa Monica
and ends in North Carolina.

The 210, like all even-numbered freeways, goes west from the San Fernando Valley, through the homes of the Rose Parade, and joins Interstate 10 in the San Gabriel Valley in the east of this 4,500 square mile city. It was a god send to the trucking community. Before it was built, those guys had to take Interstate 5, the Golden State Freeway, through Los Angeles proper to go east, and you don't even want to think about that.

The construction of the 210 started simultaneously from both ends and met somewhere near the center of the whole thing. This technique of starting at the two ends of something and joining them in the middle has been used, with varying degrees of success, throughout the country,

Not so in San Diego, however.

So the construction of the 210 proceeded according to plans. However, somewhere in the process, a small earth fault line was discovered in one of the canyons that the freeway was passing through. It had not been picked up during the preliminary scans. That slowed things down a bit. After the Hollywood machine found out about this delay, they took full advantage of it and filmed a lot of the exterior parts of their highway show on the completed part west of the newly discovered fault. Eventually, the construction plans were altered to accommodate for the fault and the freeway was completed.

To understand the evolution of the freeway, it is essential to visit what is possibly the first one built. It was started shortly after the end of the second white tribal war and ran from the Home of the Rose Bowl to downtown Los Angeles proper. It was named the Arroyo Seco Parkway and was described, in the vernacular of the day as, "a leisurely drive to downtown Los Angeles". Mind you, even then, gridlock and traffic jams were becoming all too common. We had already these with the horse and buggy, all the privately owned rail companies. After the auto, it was also added to the mix.

> *We all started buying cars for REAL*
> *after that second tribal war.*
> *All that money was flying around.*

So a leisurely drive that was unfettered sounded awfully attractive.

Enter what is now Interstate 710. It was originally a state highway and was No. 7, the Pasadena Freeway. No. 11 went to Long Beach. I use to party in both cities–'7 come 11'!! Now the freeway boys want to extend the 710 farther (it's part of the Interstate system today) into what is now South Pasadena. Of course this would mean destroying more homes, displacing more people, cutting down more trees, adding more to the gridlock, etc., etc., etc. Get the picture?

> *The highway lobby is now*
> *driven solely by profit.*
> *Everything else be damned..*

As the train systems disappeared, the ribbons of concrete took their place. A pearl of moviedom called "Who Framed Roger Rabbit" tells the story best about the first freeway built in Los Angeles along with the necessary destruction of the mass transit system.

"There'll be gas stations and freeways everywhere—it will be glorious".

Yeh, Right!!!

By the time the Pomona Walnut exchange was constructed—it has 5 levels of concrete ribbons soaring through the air—bands and great pomp were used to open them for official use. The television cameras were there. Today, very little or no fanfare is used. When they are completed, they just start being used. When you're in the San Diego area, check out the skyway across Mission Valley that joins the north and south rims of that valley. It's another great ribbon of concrete in the sky.

The design of the modern freeway is excellent, well graded and easy to navigate. For my money, the best of all that is San Diego and Los Angeles is the path between the two cities themselves. The only other freeway I've driven that compares to this road is the freeway between Olympia and Seattle, Washington. When roads are built well, cars practically drive themselves. Cruise control was designed just for this type of road.

Now that we're all dashing about the continent at 70+mph, in rain or shine, we will eventually realize that most of us would rather be traveling in real leisure—

Translated as NOT DRIVING AT ALL

Talk to people from other parts of the planet about how they travel. The car is there but most travel by train or bus, that old collective idea.

Not even the airplane can compare to the ability to move more humans over a greater space and for less cost.

The bicycle, a truly personal mode of transport is used by another huge block of the human family. It uses very little oil. Little wonder, we only see it during the races. Count the number of car commercials and then see how many bicycle commercials you see.

The white guys who started us out on this path to build ribbons of concrete are all dead now. It's time we buried their idea with their bodies. Turn the freeways over to the truckers—they keep the economy of our young country working anyway. Put most of us non-truckers back into trains and buses with all the electronic toys we all like. That way, we won't be hitting little old ladies because we're too busy talking on the cell phone while we're trying to drive.

Use the Internet and talk to the rest of the planet. The Russians put transit systems in any city that had reached a population of one million. Now that's planning. Even Spain, frozen in time, has high-speed rail. Most of Europe has high-speed rail and we won't even mention the Japanese and the Germans. These guys have working models of trains that travel on air—no friction, no heat, with speeds above 300 mph, on the ground—closed systems—no cross traffic at all. Now that the Chinese had decided to industrialize, they've asked the Germans to help them build a maglev system in that vast country of theirs.

More intelligent that building ribbons of concrete in the sky.

Right in Front of These Eyes

He was kind, took an interest in me. In those days his job title was janitor. On this day, he offered to show me this thing.

My dad worked in this city and this was where his job was. When my mom and I came to visit on the weekends, I had the run of the place. For a 12-year-old, it was like a private Disneyland.

The area we were looking at on this day didn't have too many lights but like the rest of the building, it had been wired for electricity when we started using that form of lighting. This building was a part of my white brother's his-story that he's just now getting credit for. My father tried to get his flock to save this thing, but their interest was elsewhere. They were distracted and lost control of this part of their his-story. Later on, that part of the city was reshaped into other uses by my white brother and this thing disappeared from the planet.

The part of the building where we were on this day had been built with bricks—thousands and thousands of bricks—and they were red. Where I grew up, the brick is used to build lots of stuff, some a lot better than others. What I was now seeing was done very, very well. Had this thing been preserved, it would still look the same today. Besides, it was underground, away from the forces of the planet.

> *On this planet,*
> *if you want to preserve something*
> *for a very long time,*
> *build it with stone,*
> *build it in the earth or underground.*

The whole area had a semi-circular shape. I could see many openings in the wall that were shaped like doorways. However, there were no doors in these openings which had arches over where a door would normally be found. When I looked inside one of these little rooms, it reminded me of a cell that I had seen in a movie. There was a broken wooden chair in the cell I looked in. It was covered with lots of dust. One of the legs was missing but it was still standing upright. It looked a lot like the chairs I had seen in a lot of the small country churches when I tagged along with the father when he was working. He had traveled a lot before he came to the place.

As my eyes grew accustomed to the dim light, I looked at the floor. It too was made of red brick. However, the floor was not level. It had a shape like the arches in the little rooms. I walked over the arch in the floor. It wasn't very high, but it was almost as wide as the whole room. The part of the humped floor that went away from the little rooms disappeared into the ground. That part of the arched floor was not too far from the door we had come through when we went into the sub-basement of this very old church.

The Presbyterians had built it before the un-Civil War. They were from Scotland.

The sanctuary was on the second floor. The ground floor had classrooms, offices, bathrooms and the like. I remember going to some functions on the ground floor that didn't involve the worship service. I got dressed up once and went to something with my mom and dad in the middle of the week. My mom had her own profession, so she and I didn't go to this place during the week much. We lived in our permanent home some 80+miles to the south in a neighboring state

When I was there, is was the Friday evening and Saturday before the Sunday service. We just had the one. Unlike the Baptists, who spent the whole Sunday at church, Methodists of the day generally left and went home after that one service. This was usually around o'clock in the afternoon when the one service for the week was over.

So my memories of this church where my father worked was one of exploration and adventure.

On one occasion that kind individual I mentioned earlier showed me the pipe organ that was high above the pulpit which was about 4 feet above the sanctuary floor. He told me that some of the pipes were 32 feet tall. They certainly looked like it. There were five rows of keys. I had learned how to play the piano but had never seen this many keys with all those buttons between the rows. There was another keyboard on the floor that was played with the feet. My mom knew how to play an organ, but I never mananged to learn. The wooden exterior of the organ had spires that matched the backs of the chairs in the pulpit. The bench where you sat to play the organ had carved sides and a back that looked like outside of the organ.

The chairs in the pulpit was carved to look like the outside of the organ as well. There were five of these chairs with the one in the middle being taller than the rest. The cushions on these chairs were covered in red velvet. There were two sides balconies and one back balcony surrounding the main floor of the sanctuary. There were pews under the side balconies, with stained glass windows that let in dazzling light when the sun was out.

The ends of the pews were carved to look like the organ and the chairs on the pulpit. There were three columns of pews, with two aisles between the three columns and an aisle that ran along the sides of the outside columns of pews. There were about 25 rows of pews in each column. All the pews in the center of the sanctuary also had these long pads covered in red velvet. The pews in the side balconies didn't have those red velvet pads. Those benches could be very hard. The side balconies sometimes had people in them on Sunday. The back balcony was usually empty, even on Sunday. The pews up there had black velvet cushions. It was my playground on those days. I could sit back there when I was "at church". The only time I had to sit on the main floor was during the Christmas and Easter services. My mom usually sang in the choir and on the crowded days, I sat in a pew under one of the side balconies or with the wife of the janitor. He's the man who was showing me all these parts of this magnificent church.

When the choir marched down the left and right isles on Sunday, they would go in back of the pulpit, climb the stairs and sit in the organ loft with the organist. The organ had been converted from a manual to an electric system. When electricity became all the rage, machines that had been operated by hand had motors added to them.

One of the downsides of progress is the loss of some jobs.

Another item in the church had been converted to electricity. A gigantic chandelier hung from the center of the sanctuary. It was made of solid brass. Must have weighed something frightful. The overall diameter was about 8 feet. There were four circles of lights, the largest being at the top and three smaller circles of lights beneath the uppermost. The bottom circle was the smallest and was about 2 feet in diameter with the other two above being graduated in size. Each circle of lights had a space of a foot or so between them.

One Saturday morning I was exploring the building as usual and came upon that man I've mentioned before. He was changing some of the bulbs in this chandelier. He had lowered it down to pew level and showed me the cable that held up this collection of light bulbs. The cable was bigger than one of my legs. There must have been over 100 bulbs on the largest circle of this chandelier. He told me that before electricity, candles and oil lamps had been used on the same fixture. After he changed all the burned out bulbs, he went toward the back balcony and climbed the stairs toward the bell tower. Somewhere up there he made it to where the mechanism was that made it possible to lower that chandelier. I had been standing next to it while he was changing the bulbs and now it was slowly getting higher and higher above me. Soon it was back in its usual position.

On the day I went into the sub-basement with my guide, he told me what it had been used for. He said that runaway slaves had been housed in those little rooms as they escaped the apartheid system that was the rule where they had come from. He also told me that the tunnel had gone from under the church toward the Ohio River. To the runaway slave, the Ohio River was a physical boundary between freedom and slavery.

Some of them spent time in this station of the underground railroad, and now, here this part of that railroad was right in front of these eyes.

Just Whose Brain's in There Anyway?

By the time Andy was just under five, Mark had realized that this child he and Barbara had produced would forever be surprising him with his thinking. Although many kids can read at three, four and five these days, even his now ex had begun to notice the unusual things that a boy of Andy's apparent age talked about. Dottie, Barbara's best friend, was crazy about Andy and was always asking about what college his father was going to send Andy to. His son was not even in kindergarten yet, and she was talking college? Just what was going on here? Just who was this guy pretending to be his son? Where had he come from? Could he be an alien from some unknown galaxy?

Mark English was now realizing that he had a full-time job on his hands. Barbara had been as helpful as she could, but she was not up to the job of being a mother and a business woman at the same time. She had the flair for business, he had the flair for being a parent. By the time of the separation, Mark had gotten use to Andy's unusual requests; he was also used to explaining his son to the usually stunned listener. Most people found it difficult to deal with such questions from a body that looked as if it had just completed potty training. Mark had long ago given up on the fantasy that his son would make it to the NBA or the NFL. Andy would be pint-sized most of his life for sure, but he more than made up for his small stature with that brain in his head. So even Mark was stopped in his tracks when Andy asked him the following question one Sunday morning during breakfast.

"Dad, am I old enough to be issued a passport?"

"Don't know, dude. Don't think so, however. It's probably got something to do with being old enough to sign contracts and all that usually starts around your 18th birthday or so. Do you have business somewhere outside these borders.?"

He really couldn't answer his question and was extremely curious as to where this was all going.

"I'd like to go to the Serengeti" came Andy's reply.

Feeling like he was being led, Mark had to ask "What's happening in the Serengeti?"

"I want to go to see some ostriches where they live".

Genuinely interested in anything his son talked about, Mark inquired as to this apparent new interest of Andy's, for his son had never brought up the subject about animals and things of this nature before.

"I read in a book at the library that ostriches buried their heads in the sand when they were frightened. Then I saw a film on television and it didn't say anything at all about ostriches hiding their heads in the sand. The teevee showed a lot about the mating dance, egg laying and how they protect and raise the young, but didn't say anything about the hiding of heads in the sand. Nothing at all." He then continued "I thought I should go to the Serengti where they live to see for myself."

Mark had to remind himself that he was having a conversation with a four+-year-old who thought like someone with great age under his belt. His logic was inescapable. When presented with conflicting information, analyze the situation for yourself. Consequently, he was not at all prepared for what Andy said next.

"It sounds like hiding their head in the sand is something people do".

Turkey Month, 2002

"Our world changed forever"–a statement used to introduce the name of a fellow employee who left us on September 11, 2001.

I'm intrigued by the use of the possessive pronoun our. Is this an American 'our' or a human 'our'?

In most instances, those of us born in this nation-state tend to forget that we share this planet with countless others. Those of our species who have chosen to migrate to these shores voluntarily have a better understanding of what potential this nation really represents.

This standard of living that we Americans worship exacts a terrible planetary price from us all–including those who don't even live here. During the past 25 years alone this nation has, for one reason or another, found cause to invade, persecute or otherwise bully smaller nations in this hemisphere. Other nations on the other side of the planet have not been spared the "wrath" of the one remaining super-power. These actions were taken, ostensibly, to protect the 'American way of life'.

With power and strength comes a certain amount of responsibility.

The present occupant of the white house has said that we are a country 'awakened to danger'. Does this mean we were not aware of the danger that other members of our species had to face when we took it upon ourselves to invade their homelands for the trivial reasons we conceived over the past half century? I think not.

We hear the phrase "God bless America" a lot in these days of remembrance and during the days of the actual event itself. Does this statement imply that this god withhold his blessing from everyone else on the planet? We are told that a supreme being created our species. Does this song imply that somehow this creator holds this country more special than any other? If so, those of you with children know this is not a very good practice—favoring one child over another—something about sibling rivalry.

Such an attitude is a typical, myopic American point of view. Granted, we seem to have made life easier here, but so have many other places outside these borders. The comfort and contentment one feels about his or her life is entirely subjective. There are billions of our species that don't necessarily want to come here. Is this why the media machine only seems to be able to show you scenes of misery and deprivation in other lands? Talk about hidden agendas.

This "standard of living" that Americans worship has come at the expense of many others on our home world. We are 1/25th of the planet's population and we use more than 50% of the total resources of the entire planet to support our 'lifestyle' or 'the American way of life'. Somehow we've convinced ourselves that this is the way our species is supposed to live.

While this belief of ours is noble and wrapped in sentiment, it may not necessarily be true for all members of the human family. I once worked with a woman who was born and raised in Poland. She had come to America (as outsiders call this place) and made the observation that it was, in her exact words, "one fuckin' hard place to live".

As more and more of our citizens are falling through the cracks—not able to afford basic housing, healthcare or the means to travel in the accepted method—it becomes imperative that we analyze our methods of operating and our core concepts as applied to life on this planet, in general, and in our homeland, specifically.

For all intent and purposes, we have created a permanent underclass, an American version of the untouchables. The next time you have a conversation with someone from India, Pakistan, Bangladesh or Japan, ask them about the untouchables in their lands. Such a development in our land invalidates the tenets of that christian religion that many rave about. The majority of the wealth of the nation resides in the hands of such a small number. The general public (those not in the wealthy class) can be called upon to support this underclass for only so long. That time is coming to an end even now.

While the power elite are focused on war, the rest of the population must deal with the decaying structures that support the system.

The America you grew up with has been murdered.

What is now evolving is for all of us to determine.

Suburbs

Why do you fear me, what frightens you so?
I do wish you'd tell me for I'd really like to know.

It's really difficult to function in an air so unclear,
filled with the storm clouds created by your panic and fear.

It is the color of my eyes or the texture of my hair,
Or is the color of my skin or the clothes I choose to wear?

There seems to be no pattern indicating intelligent thinking,
just the ramblings of a confused mind after too much drinking.

Why do you run from me so, I'm not after your life,
I have my own, thank you, and no, I'm not after your wife.

Me thinks it's yourself you really fear.

Hollywood
1971

Did We Miss Something?

In this ongoing experiment called America, it has become widely accepted that it's possible that a majority of us are not taking part in the "governmental process"—voting being the individual's recognition of that process and its connection to their individual realities. Apparently the turning away from voting is going on elsewhere. Those guys over in the mother country, nee The United Kingdom, are feeling the same way it seems. I recently saw this clip that involved a conversation with a young female adult who refuted the notion that no one was voting because they weren't interested. Her response: "That's rubbish. We just don't see any difference between the conservatives and labor."

My immediate thought was "Chil', tell me something I don't already know."

The locals are staying away from the polls in droves. They're interested in things at their level, where it fits in with their own realities. Much of what is presented to them on the national level has the aura of illusion, not being real. Those that do participate do so out of drone-like habit—supporting a reality that is dying, but they don't see it. Besides, many of us also remember what happened to the Kennedys and King. When the citizenry does get involved, the frightened power elite reacts with predictable and swift violence. Some white males can be so insecure.

Then you can imagine my surprise when I hear about another group of the species family who recently went to the polls to vote. Reports were coming across planetary news sources that around 85% of these guys went to the polls. The overall response was so great that the voting officials had to extend the voting times in several locations.

What a concept!!

I also learned that this same part of the family grants the vote at age 16. I really don't know if this function is extended to females at that age because this voting took place in one of those societies where the female side of our species is restricted.

What really caught my attention was an additional bit about the officials taking voting materials to the inmates of their penal system.

Who are these people and where did they come from? How long have they been a part of the human family and why haven't I heard about all this before? How come we don't do that here as well?

So apparently these guys must think differently about crime.

We take that voting right away once a citizen is reclassified as a felon. They have felons as do we but they keep them on the voting roles.

So, where is this place, you say?

It's one of those bad guys you're not supposed to like—they're different, they're not Christian and they don't do what we want them to. They've made their displeasure at some of the things we've done known publicly and they've stuck to their guns, sometimes literally. They've put up with America's abuse that we've heaped upon them in our short his-story and gone on about their business, in spite of all our efforts to the contrary.

It's Persia. Oops, I'm sorry, that it's pre-Christian name. It's modern name is Iran.

Did we miss something?

Slavery is a Hard Habit to Break

As the human-based empires began to die, it became obvious to the powers of each that slavery was excessively expensive. It was this recognition that drove the second industrial revolution with its emphasis on machinery. However, it soon became apparent that the human being would still be needed to man these new machines that increased the overall wealth of the elite.

Minimum wage-based slavery became the order of the day as the industrial juggernaut set sail on the planet. Those societies that were not interested in the industrial prowess of the west or who didn't instantly copy their methods were classified as second rate and their home-grown philosophy and approach to life became suspect. When such societies embarked on political paths different from those developed by the west, they immediately became cast in the role as enemy.

Slavery, as a human concept,
is as old as human societies themselves.

The tribes of Europe had been taught that difference meant inferior. During the dark ages they had come to be believe that the entire planet was theirs for the taking. All other members of the human family were subjected to slavery whenever and wherever the white male cast his military and religious ethic.

As more and more of the human family have begun to **not** accept the role of slave, the former slave masters have been forced to accept these changes in the mentality of their former slaves.

The descendants of the English Empire, who started the American Empire, used slavery, as did the mother country. The first people used were the indentured servants, who were citizens of the British Empire having some debt to pay, those from the penal system and those who had fallen from grace for various reasons. These white slaves, for the most part, worked off their servitude and took off into the vastness of the New World to build their own empires. Some of them grew into large concerns. The original humans who lived on this continent prior to the arrival of the slaveholders didn't take too well to being cast as slaves and fled to other parts of the continent, away from those who would be slave masters. Eventually, the American Empire would reduce their numbers to what it considered a manageable state.

To solve the need for slaves, those from other parts of the planet were imported to drive the economic engine based on slavery. The African slave was the perfect answer. He was the descendant of the evil Cain, was seen as sub-human and knew neither the language nor the land. He was the perfect answer to the problem of the day. In later times, other members of the species would serve the role of slave in other parts of the American Empire, but the mentality and pattern of treatment was the same.

As times changed and the former slaves began to throw off the acceptance of the slave role, the previous slave master would resort to various methods to reassert his role as slave master in order to maintain his-story and his mental balance.

It has always been easy for black males to become preachers—this is a role that he can exploit for his own gain and also not be seen as a threat to the white male who believed him to be a pacifier of the former slave.

> ***You'll get your reward in heaven.***
> ***I'm getting mine now on your backs.***

In our present day, white America has had to confront its own past and the part it played in the maintenance of the slave system. Since importing was expensive, it would much easier and cheaper to increase the slave count by producing them here at home. Consequently, the role of slave father has recently been discussed concerning one of the premier icons of the American Empire. The claims of democracy ring hollow around our planet.

> ***You can cook my food, cut my lawn,***
> ***clean my home, drive my buggy,***
> ***watch after my kids or even give birth to my kids,***
> ***who in turn will add to my wealth,***
> ***but don't have an opinion.***

As the American Empire began to form its personality, the principals of democracy were espoused to give notice to the mother country that the rejects of the Mother Empire would set their own course in his-story. Since the mother country was about to abolish slavery, the question of its continued use in the American Empire eventually came up for discussion. When the status of these slaves was determined in the formation of this new empire, their value as human beings was placed at the fraction of three-fifths.

Personally, I've always been intrigued as to how and why this particular fraction was discerned. Why not two-thirds, one quarter or even one-half. I do believe that percentages were being used in those times. Why didn't the figure of 75% get used in this assigning of human-ness? At the end of the beginning of America, the slavery question stayed around until the so-called end of that system with the emancipation proclamation.

The quality of the lives of these ex-slaves has changed considerably but the atmosphere in which these glacial changes have taken place is still the same. In this new millennium, white America still needs a scape-goat upon which it cans cast its own problems. That accusatory finger is still being pointed in my direction.

As I said earlier, slavery is a hard habit to break.

It Be Weird!

Eve and Pandora are the same story told by different tribes.

So, that bit about the "evils of the world"
was just told in another fashion
for entirely different purposes.

The Greeks knew that the gods had set up Pandora. She was a pawn in the game the gods had with man. Like Eve, her action takes place at the "birth" of man, however, the Greek version put man on a path that made him a challenger to the gods. The interpretation of the other version was touted by the church and became, for many, *the* creation story of choice. Don't forget, like Zeus and other immortals, the god in the Hebrew stories used a mortal female for his offspring. The fact that it was done by remote control does not change the fact that it was a story that had been told before. Nothing new here, after all.

The Eve version, when looked at without the usual company line interpretation, has some very interesting facts that raise more questions than provide answers.

- The culprit in this particular story was the serpent. It spoke to Eve and contradicted what this particular immortal had told both her and Adam after he had finished "creating" them. Does this mean that all other creatures were capable of talking to members of our species? That doesn't seem to have been mentioned. Just the serpent. Weird.

- Why was it necessary for the "creator" to bring the man in to name the other creatures that he had "created"? How could Adam know the names of the other planetary beings if he, himself, had just been "created"? Weird.

- What happened to Adam's brain? If he had been given certain instructions at the same time as Eve, why didn't he refuse when she "offered him that forbidden knowledge"? Are males really that weak minded? (Sometimes I think so!)

- Why did the immortal accept Adam's lame excuse that it was "her fault"?

- Why didn't he just punish Eve and leave Adam alone, since it appears that Adam didn't talk to the serpent. Bad tactics on the part of the immortal. Don't punish the whole class for the actions of one. *(Sound familiar?)*

- The creation lines go—"Let us make man in our image". These two pronouns are PLURAL words. Only one god has ever been mentioned, if I remember. What's with this "us" and "our"? Weird.

- If Eve had not talked to the serpent, would our species have developed? Wasn't the species created to reproduce itself, or did this particular immortal want to keep producing our kind by himself (We've been told that the immortal was male. How come?) No male creature on this planet reproduces its own kind, just females. There's something wrong with this picture. Weird.

- So after the expulsion, our newlyweds set about starting a family. Along the way, one of their sons is supposed to have killed his brother. The motive for this act was directly related to the actions of the immortal, who's still hanging around for some reason. Was the whole family on probation? Weird.

- After the immortal discovers the foul deed, the remaining son is banished to the Land of Nod. ***Where?????***

Capital punishment came much later.

When places on our planet are given names, it indicates the presence of members of our species. No other life form does this. Just where did these Nod humans come from and why weren't we told about their "creation"?

Now that the newlyweds have lost both of their children, they are supposed to have continued producing to fill the earth. This can't be in balance because this would mean that our species is the result of an incestuous relation between members of the same family. Since there were no more males other than the original one, it appears that he must have produced offspring with his wife and his own daughters in order to "fill the land". Once more sons were born, they continued "filling the land". Not a good genetic practice—extremely small gene pool.

It be weird.

The Spinal Cord's Finial

Who's doing your thinking—are you using your own brain,
Or did you let some leader take your cerebrum out and leave it in the
rain?

Is your thinking fuzzy—has the smog gone to your head,
Do you look around for someone dynamic to agree with what he said?

Are you eager for heroes—do you need them to identify
Are you looking for a saver to take you up into the sky?

Do you find them on teevee—on the financial page,
Or are you deluded into struggling for the highest wage?

Who said you have to—uncle sam, kousin karl or vickie,
Shoring up these tenets can get to be rather sticky.

Growing up requires discarding old ideas and ritual,
For blindly following forever turns one into something quite pitiful.

I love you, have no fear of me 'cause my thinking you cannot see
You don't have to hate because you're insecure
I have my own job to do and that's for sure.

Always challenge your knowledge, challenge your beliefs.
Unchanging dogma, rigid thinking and, lately, tunnel vision
Create the atmospheres that keep our cultures brief.

Venice
1978

The Empire Game

Most of us know of or remember learning something about human empires during our time spent in whatever school we were taken to by our parents or guardians. A lot of this human history was rather boring, at least it was to me at the time. High school is a time of enormous physical and emotional change. The last thing any of us would be interested in at such a time would be the exploits of some dead people who couldn't possibly have any bearing on what was going on in our lives at the time.

For me, I didn't really become interested in this subject until well into my college years and only after my exposure to a style of learning introduced to my by someone I mentioned elsewhere in these writings.

As empires go, Americans would probably mention England or the United Kingdom, as it was often called. Because of the particular love-hate relationship with this particular empire, many of our nation would think of it first. However, the Roman Empire is a constant topic in many areas of discussion. During these particular times, many references to the similarities of our system and our present predicaments are constantly being made by the pundits of the day. The omnipresence of the Judeo-Christian ethic is responsible for this outlook.

As a rule, all human societies have practiced the art or science of building empires for various reasons. Hundreds have come and gone in what collective recorded history of our species we retain to this day. There are also many legends of great empires that have vanished from the planetary scene.

For the most part, our young nation is the direct result of the actions and wars carried out by three human empires—England, France and Spain. A fourth one, Russia, was not involved in a military or warfare sense, but was also a contributor to the development of the American empire.

In various sections of what we now call our country, these three now-dead empires took pot shots at each other for reasons quite similar to those that we used in our on-going battles with the now deceased Russian empire. It's now a federation.

Since we Americans know very little about empires other than the ones mentioned above, I'd like to take the opportunity to start with some of the earliest human empires that we know of.

The nation of Sumer is an ancient society that might qualify as an early example of a human empire–influence exerted by one group over one or several other neighboring groups. In most cases, past or present, alliances or empires are formed for mutual trade and protection from larger and more powerful groups.

However, the predominant pattern is one of military conquest of one group over another for various reasons. The resulting situation that is a direct outcome of this military action is one of subjugation of the conquered group.

Alexander the Great is one of Western man's favorite topics when this topics comes up for discussion. He is seen as one of the progenitors of our present system and many of the tenets of government that we aspire to come from, ostensibly, from this empire. Many of the cultures mentioned in the bible were empires of varying sizes. Because they were usually competitors with the empire of the Judeans, not much of a positive nature about these empires was recorded in this book. Usually the destruction of this or that empire was all that was mentioned.

The previously mentioned Roman Empire is the next step in the evolution of the so-called Western style. Since both Greece and Rome were military dictatorships, it doesn't take a rocket scientist to figure out why we operate in the same fashion with our own empire today.

Tourists to other parts of the planet will tell the untraveled reader of the remains of other human empires that did not contribute to the formation of our country. Contributions from these dead empires are now being made in the form of humans from these places. These older societies had come and gone long before those empires that formed us gained power. Many Asians and Indian empires flowered and died unknown to the mind of Western man. In our time, this information has come to light. Many from the west have become interested in this part of human history and citizens from these cultures are uncovering their own pasts as well. As a result we are all growing in our collective knowledge about our species.

Our attention has recently been turned toward the empires to the south of our country that flowered and died before we the United States came into existence. The descendants of these human empires make up major portions of our present system.

The American psyche is, at this point in time, constructed from the history of the empire games of Europe, which the English won, so to speak. In modern terms, their empire lasted the longest. Before its death it was, by all accounts, the largest empire ever operated by humans.

The Spanish were the first to recognize the futility and the cost of running such a venture on this continent. Their departure from the empire stage was hastened by the English in that celebrated naval battle in the channel. That victory, however, was actually caused by the planet and the weather that arose that day. The fact that the Spanish were not good ship builders was another factor that contributed to their defeat. They had insisted on building those large and lumbering galleons that were not very maneuverable. The English, on the other hand, used those Dutch-designed vessels that were smaller, lighter and more agile. This particular sea battle has been celebrated in many movies and other productions of the printed and visual media.

The Spanish empire was sustained largely by the wealth taken from the South American continent and those empires that were dying or had died prior to the arrival of the conquistadors. Much of the gold that was taken from that part of the world ended up in Spain. A lot of it also ended up at the bottom of the oceans between here and there. As a result of the sudden influx of such wealth, their economy was overheated and started on its way to the inevitable collapse and the end of their empire. As more and more of the former colonies began to demand independence, it only hastened the end of the once powerful Spanish empire. Their legacy today is the language that remains. However, like many others of our species that are now undoing many of the negative influences of the empire builders, those peoples of the southern American continent are rediscovering that own identities.

The French lasted a bit longer in the empire game but eventually had to yield to the realization that such ventures are too expensive to maintain. They, like the English, contributed major portions of the landmass that now calls itself America. Like all colonial powers, that had taken major portions of the continent from which to draw mineral wealth to run their particular empire. They eventually sold their holdings to the fledging nation calling itself America. Their cultural influence is ever present in our time today. They not only left their names but also part of their legal system, which differed from that of the English. These two former adversaries reached a "Mexican standoff" in what is now called Canada. In this nation they seemed to have settled their old tribal differences somewhat and are living in a peaceful arrangement.

Other members of our species went through empire phases but did not export them on a planetary basis, as did the tribes of Europe.

The American empire, now dying, was started primarily to announce to the older European empires that we would build an empire on this side of the planet. As a result, the Americans took the all islands of the Pacific and 'liberated' the islands of the Philippines after the Spanish empire went broke. The islands of the West Indies were considered to be "under the protection" of America, but were largely ignored because there were composed primarily of black humans who were the descendants of slaves that had left America. The island nation of Cuba was part of this empire until they decided to shape their own destiny. Despite all its apparent 'wealth and power' the white males who control the economy of America have not been able to prevent the people of that island from continuing this change.

The standard of living that America enjoys is a direct descendant of the standard of living attained by the empires of Europe after they colonized great portions of the planet. The African and South American continents provided the financial foundation for this standard of living. The American empire continued this rape of these continents well into the 20th century. It is only at the end of the 20th and beginning of the 21st centuries that we have seen major shifts in these colonial attitudes. Most, if not all of the original nations of the African continent have regained their independence. They have, in many cases, returned to their original names prior to the arrival of this white child and are in the process of uncovering their own unique identities. The same process will eventually occur in the South American continent. Despite the dominance of the religion and culture left by the colonials, the languages and foundations of the original cultures are slowly being uncovered.

Even the planet has gotten into the act of ending this empire game. A medium-sized cinder giant named Pinatubo decided the fate of the

American military presence in the Philippines. While the Philippine senate was actually debating whether to renew the leases on those two military bases that our nation had there, the mountain covered them in ash and made the question moot. When Prince Charles handed over the last part of the British Empire to the Chinese, it rained on him. That little military foray off the coast of Argentina was the last gasp of the now deceased British Empire. It appears that the Japanese and Russians are slowly coming to some sort of agreement about those little islands they've been squabbling over. Another example of planetary involvement was the creation of an island, a continual process, in the area of Iceland. It seems that this newly forming island became the center of debate over who would eventually own it—Iceland or some other country. While this debate raged, the island blew up and disappeared from the face of the earth. Question settled.

There are ever increasing rumblings from the citizens of the islands of the Pacific that past injustices now have to be addressed. It is doubtful that the citizens of Puerto Rico will decide to become the 51st state. They may like the relationship with this place as it is, and they're independent of this place in the bargain. They have area codes, zip codes and all the rest of the technology that we here in the mainland expect. Why confuse the issue by getting mixed up with the insane political process, stolen elections and all, that are present here at this time. Leave well enough alone.

It appears that on this planet the empire game is finally over.

Hallelujah!!!!!

"Tim, meet Jim".

The term is civil disobedience, not terrorism.

Certain individuals and groups of individuals have always disobeyed the rules of many different societies. The Republican system of the Greeks ordered a malcontent to drink hemlock in an effort to curtail his civil disobedience. Some of the tenets from that system found their way into the United States Constitution when the founders used civil disobedience to tell George III and his boys to take a hike.

**It was time for this form of operating
to start toward its end.**

Along the way in the growth of America, we've all been witness to many different kinds of civil disobedience, from train robbers to robber barons, from legal and illegal gangs to political burglars.

We've all just witnessed the death of someone conveniently classified as a terrorist, but whose act was really one of civil disobedience. The horror of this particular event is the fact that it happened in the middle of our own country and was carried out by one of our own children. The indiscriminate death of innocents also contributes to the memory. Talk to the citizens of any country outside these borders. They'll tell you a thing or two about civil obedience. It hasn't always been called terrorism, you know.

So, as a matter of contrast, I offer the reader an American act of civil disobedience in which no was killed. In fact, the only death associated with this particular act was that of the person who did the deed, and that death didn't come about until some time after this unusual act of civil disobedience.

This particular person, whose name was Jim, attacked a building, a Veterans' Hospital in West Los Angeles. Like that building over in Oklahoma City, this hospital was constructed with public funds. This military hospital is the same part of town as is UCLA. It was relatively new at the time. The hospital compound was originally set up for use in the second of my white brothers' tribal wars. A lot of the older buildings in the complex have wonderful wooden architecture, lots of wood with ornate shapes and such. This new building was of a later time—glass, polished aluminum and granite or some such stone. I seem to remember 10 or 11 floors, maybe more—Wadsworth was the formal name. Over on Wilshire Boulevard the buildings were considerably taller.

The day of this event started out as countless others—a grounds man was mowing one of the many plots of grass at this location. Several people were sitting scattered throughout the lobby of the hospital. They had gotten there early to beat the usual lines that seem to be at hospitals. There was a television set hanging from the ceiling but it wasn't on. On another wall of the lobby was the usual official plaque listing the date of construction and the people involved with all this. Jimmy Carter's picture was hanging on one of these lobby walls as well. Ronald Reagan had just been elected but Jimmy's picture was still up on the wall of this Veterans' Hospital. Somehow the staff hadn't gotten around to replacing Jimmy's picture with one of Ronald.

The relatively quiet of the morning was suddenly shattered by the sound of a jeep motor revving up followed by loud crashes of breaking glass and bending metal. A citizen had just backed his jeep into the lobby of this building. The driver of the vehicle got out. He was dressed in military garb and was armed with what looked like a standard issue GI rifle, a side arm and another weapon used in war made by the other superpower of the day. The next thing everyone realized that they were being asked to please leave the lobby.

It was said they split immediately.

After they departed, the citizen shot up the lobby with that gun made over in Russia.

This particular citizen was having a running battle with the operators of the building he had just attacked. At the time, he was gradually losing his hearing and nothing was being done about it. They were stalling and that bit they told him about his records being 'lost in a fire' in a storage facility didn't help matters any. To further rub salt into an open wound—that facility fire happened in his home state, even in his hometown, I do believe.

They had balked. He was too outspoken. He hadn't gotten the medical attention the facility had been constructed to provide. He was also talking, a lot, about a chemical named Agent Orange being responsible for his hearing loss. Apparently, this citizen had been sprayed with this defoliant while he was in a war zone called Vietnam. Predictably, when the word about what had just happened got out, the electronic media had shown up. The citizen had taken the opportunity to report his views and his reasons for the "attack" when they arrived to cover this strange incident. It was covered by most of the stations of the area and was being talked about on the airwaves that morning.

The United States doesn't have a federal police force, as do our neighbors to the south. As a consequence, the operators of the building had to call in the local constabulary-the now infamous LAPD. Their reputation at that time was not too sterling and it has only gone down hill since then. The citizen was duly arrested and ultimately charged with—are you ready—'threatening the life of the president', who at the time was no longer in office.

Since we continue to refer to these elected individuals as Mr. President after they've left office, I suppose that was a valid charge. However, after the jurisdictional legal dust had cleared, this citizen spent a very small amount of time being incarcerated for this act of civil disobedience, less than a week. A few months later, however, this citizen's wife came home from work one day to find her husband in their bed. He was no longer alive.

At the medical inquest into his death, which didn't come about for a great deal of time, it was determined that he had taken his own life. Although the original contents of the decedent's stomach could no longer be located, the records indicated that the only substances present at the time were chloral hydrate, alcohol and some foodstuffs. On the bedside nightstand a bottle of some kind of bourbon whiskey had been found along with some pills, whose makeup were never determined nor recorded. The chloral hydrate was the most likely substance that could be blamed for his death but the amount found was insufficient. Apparently one would have to ingest nearly ½ pound of the stuff to cause death. Only a few grams were found in this case.

And now, a little side discussion about drinking.

Those of you in the audience who choose to use the drug alcohol and do so with moderation usually have a particular brand to which you may be loyal. Visiting your favorite watering hole with any regularity makes it easy for the bartender to fix your "usual" and in most cases, it's a call brand. Loyalty to your favorite drug.

This particular individual had a yen for a particular brand of Scotch. Nothing else—just this one brand of Scotch. He was also NOT a pill taker. Hated it. The owners of that building had kept prescribing pills for him to take for the various stresses that had come to bear on his life prior to this act of civil disobedience. My own experiences with the medical system in this land do indicate an overwhelming propensity in favor of prescribing pills for everything, ad nauseum.

So at the medical inquest when it was reported that pills were found at the bedside, I knew that things were not quite, shall we say, kosher. What really told me the truth about the whole thing was that the bottle of alcohol found at the bedside was NOT scotch. I do remember that it was a brand of cheap bourbon whiskey. However, scotch had not been found.

The total effect of the delayed legal proceedings and the final inquest was to totally discredit the thinking process of the individual.

> *The only difference between the citizen named Jim and the citizen named Tim was their style.*

Both were trained by the military, both had been disappointed with their country in more ways than one, and both were educated. Being white males, both had expected and had gotten excellent benefits from this system. Both had excellent mental faculties not easily dismissed as "crazy" and both had taken this particular path. A lot has changed since Jim committed his act and Tim got our attention with his act. Both met their death-one with covert actions and one with great pomp and circumstance. So wherever they are, I'd like to introduce them to each other.

"Tim, meet Jim."

Four Winds

A part of me went east and a part of me went west and don't you
believe that either part is better or one is the best.

Lies may come and lies may go,
but freedom is the only truth to know.

A part of me went north and a part of me went south, and remember-
ing this past will help us find out what we're all about.

Lies may come and lies may go,
but freedom is the only truth to know.

The things we're told may not be so and myths of today were truths
long ago; soon the lies of today will be no more and the strength of the
golden days will be as before.

Lies may persist and seem never to go,
but freedom is the only truth to know.

Look closely at what you've been taught, to see if it's the grand lie
you've bought; ask your cast-down neighbor to recall the knowledge of
old that can benefit us all.

Lies don't last forever, and one day they just get up and go,
and freedom will still be the only truth to know.

Sylmar
1982

The Check's in the Mail

The mail was late today, don't know why. It's usually here between 10 and 11 a.m. but today it didn't show up until almost 5 p.m. We've been getting a lot of different carriers on this route lately, but that's not what I wanted to talk about.

When the mail did arrive, it was about the usual amount-

- two magazine-sized things (one a catalogue)
- a folded manila-type envelop from a meat company
- five business-size envelops (two were bills)
- one post card from a friend traveling back to his home from a trip to Arizona
- two book offer post cards
- and a folded, letter-sized thing with perforations on three sides.

The perforations on this last piece were across the top and down both sides. The fourth side was a fold in the middle of a standard-size sheet of paper-tear off the sides and top and you can read what's printed on the inside. It looked a lot of those mailings we get from entities asking for donations or telling you that you *may* have won some money. This particular folded and perforated thing was from the IRS.

I had heard that the citizenry was to be getting something from Foggy Bottom, but they've been in such a real fog here of late, I really don't know what to believe from that lot. After getting this thing opened, I discovered that it was indeed an announcement that I was to be receiving some funds "as part of the immediate tax relief".

Relief from what? As defined by whom?

Now I know of many of our citizens who don't file income taxes, so these folk won't be getting any tax relief. Some of these folk seem to be living decent lives-they work and pay for the things they want and need. Of course, many other of our citizens don't pay taxes because they are prevented by circumstance or choice of occupation. So these citizens won't be getting any of this relief either.

The notice went on to explain that the amount I am to receive is based on what monies I sent the IRS in a previous tax year. Since keeping track of taxes paid is their primary job, they should have the most accurate records of what I've paid into the system prior to this point.

At this point, I'd like to ask this question.

Why not just send out the check with a small note added somewhere in the printed, perforated form, telling me the wheres and what fors about this paltry sum I'm getting from this fractured government? Too many other companies seem to be able to save money and get their message across to us.

What I need is relief from is the bureaucratic bullshit and wasteful procedures performed in Foggy Bottom.

The Reactive Bank

I have an idea that the habit of reacting violently to unexpected change is probably something that comes with being human. It could also be something that each culture teaches an individual, especially males.

I mention this only as a back drop to something that occurred during my college years.

By custom and law, blacks and whites were made to live in two different worlds. We recognized this fact and went about our lives in spite of it. Most whites were totally oblivious to our comings and goings. Some still are. In most cases they stuck to the stereotypes that had been fed to them by the movie machine and the media of the nation.

Consequently, they were not prepared for the sudden start of the civil rights movement. There had been grumblings here and there during the early fifties. However, it was not until that lady decided not to move and give up her seat to a white man that things really got rolling.

She was tired that day.

It spread like wildfire. Most of the white press was covering the various happenings in whatever cities where major events took place, but the changes were going on almost everywhere, even in Frankfort, Kentucky.

This city is the capital of the state. The college I attended is there. My mother said that our white brother stuck us out in the country after the

Wilson Act of 1873 was passed establishing the land grant colleges. She always said that it was part of his desire not to be too close to us. By the time I came along, the capital city had grown out past the college and now it was smack dab in the middle of some of the most prime property in the city, if not the state. But that sort of thing has happened all over the nation.

We had a pep rally two days before this event. A major portion of the 800+student body met in the gymtorium. We heard of things happening in other places. We were told of the actions of a man named Martin Luther King who was a Baptist preacher in Montgomery, Alabama. I certainly had never heard of him. I had a preacher in my own family anway. We heard about a lady named Rosa Parks and what she had done. We were told of sit-ins in many other cities in the South. The student leaders wanted our student body to do sit-ins in Frankfort as well.

When one lives in a segregated system, there are public places that you don't go because you've learned that you're not wanted there. The rationale is unimportant because it has become custom and most people have a difficult time questioning custom, let alone changing it.

The day after the rally, many small groups of students fanned out throughout Frankfort and did the sit-in thing. My group went to a coffee shop located about ¾ of a mile from the campus on US 60. This was the main road from Lexington to Louisville before the freeway system was built.

The man at the counter was extremely nervous. I didn't do any talking; some of the seniors and appointed leaders did all that stuff. I just watched. I remember his saying something about not objecting to serving us. His hands were shaking and somewhere along in his life, he had lost a finger on his right hand.

After this rather brief exchange of views, we left. These events took place on a Saturday.

I went back to my dormitory, did some studying, went to the student union and played some pinochle with my card buddies. These card sessions usually last a couple of hours. After we packed away the cards, I had a hamburger at the geedunk and went back to dorm and went to bed.

Sunday morning, I was awakened by shouts and screams about a fire. Following the sounds, I made it to a south-facing window that looked out from the second floor in the direction of the gymtorium.

Smoke was pouring out of several windows that were open at the top and from spots under the roof. I didn't see any flames.

One other student was on the pay phone that was about seven feet from that window where several of us were standing by now. He was talking to the fire department. Then this strange look came over his face as he hung up the phone. He said that after he reported the fire, he heard the guy on the other end tell someone else, "OK–we can go now."

The firetrucks began arriving as I and some others made it up towards the gym. A large crowd was taking shape.

The first thing I noticed the firemen doing was to hack their way into the building. On a Sunday it would be closed and locked. When they got the door open, all that did was to gave air to something that had been smoldering. That completed the triangle and the smoking gun became an inferno. Almost instantly, flames began to fly out those smoking spots in the roof and windows began to shatter. When a window shattered, flames would come out afterwards. Before too long, the entire structure was involved.

We knew the gym was doomed and stood there watching. I heard one of the fireman say that he had never seen a building burn with such intensity in so many places at the same time.

After the fire was out and things had cooled down, we were able to go in and look at the results of the heat of conversion. There had been seven large I-beams that had held up the roof. They were all bent and looked like steel pretzels. Several were still attached to the walls on one end, but most had fallen to the floor. Chairs that had been used in the rally two days before were melted and crushed. Where the windows in the building had been were now gaping holes with dangling pieces of metal that had once been part of the windows. The entire roof had been melted. We were now walking on it.

The brick walls had withstood the heat but acted as a furnace for everything that had been inside. The electiric water fountain at the edge of the bleachers had been reduced to a pile of metal about one foot in height.

It was a professional job.

From that day forward, all campus functions that involved great numbers were held in Hume Hall. It was one of the oldest buildings on campus. There was a large assembly hall and stage on the second floor. My graduation ceremony was held there as well. Ordinarily it would have been held in that gymtorium, but it was gone now.

I suppose it was to intimidate or cause fear. It didn't succeed. That's all some of my white brothers seem to know. Such actions come from the reactive bank, that reptilian portion of the mind that's a holdover from those fear-laden days of tens of thousands of years ago.

Some of my white brothers haven't progressed much since then.

A Bad Review

When the final curtain came down on a little production called the dark ages, the house lights came up to reveal a starving and dying audience. The play had killed them, literally. All during the performance, there was very little to eat and a concession stand had not been included in the original theatre design. Only the house and its supporters were making any money with this show and outside vendors were not permitted in the lobby. When the play finally gave its last performance, the audience had to leave the theatre. They had been a captive audience for over nine centuries.

They began to travel, far and wide on the planet. They had been confined to their own land for such a long time. Whatever had been known about the rest of the planet had to be re-"discovered". Of course, by the time these people started doing this re-discovering, the play they had been watching had convinced them that the earth was theirs. The message from that performance was that their god 'created' them and had given them the earth to master. This drab performance had been accepted as gospel.

Once the word got out that the earth wasn't flat after all and that money could be made way out there, every Tom, Dick and Harry that could raise the capital to finance expeditions to wherever did exactly that. They went everywhere they could, even those places that were just talked about in rumors and fables.

The Portuguese were the first of the "colonials" to go forth. They were and still are excellent sailors. Soon other audience members began to do the same and before the rest of the human family knew it, we were being visited by members of this previously captive audience who were telling us that they had all the answers to this life existence and had come to save us.

From what, I might ask. I didn't know I needed saving.

An individual that was part of my life taught me this-
I have my hands full living my own life on this planet
and I don't have the means or intelligence
to save anyone else other than myself.

As we all come to the end of the "colonial" era in our collective existence, we must go through the exorcism of ridding ourselves of the tribal "religions" that were presented by the members of that captive audience of so long ago.

The members of the European tribes were kept apart from the rest of the human family against their will. When they finally were able to break the mental bonds that had held them captive for so long, they had been convinced that they had certain privileges that no other family members had. To that end they proceeded to invade and take what they considered was theirs. The opinions of the rest of the human family have never really mattered to them, even so to this very day. Much of what has come to be known has been and continues to be defined by them, even though there has never been a consensus among the family members about the directions of planetary life. To them only the attainment of wealth is an indicator of success.

In the terms of the 20th century, many members of our species are considered by them to be not successful maintaining the proper standard of living they see as the best for us all. Such terms as "third world" and "developing nations" are used to describe social systems that have been existence much longer than those who have created these new terms of social standing. There is a considerable degree of arrogance and myopia that is part of this cultural attitude in the last of the empires.

America is the bastard child of the incestuous relationships between four of the many colonial powers that existed prior to the American Revolution. As these empires went to their inevitable deaths, the American offspring learned nothing from these passing events and proceeded to repeat the mistakes of its progenitors.

Since the monetary foundation of what is called Western Civilization was built on the mineral wealth that was taken from invaded lands, the descendants of the original inhabitants of those invaded lands are now beginning to call for an accounting.

A side effect of the suppression of the talents of the tribes of Europe during the Dark Ages is a lingering fear of poverty. The American descendants of those early European tribe members are obsessed with the acquisition of wealth, at all costs. To that end, the American system is the only human system that makes reference to a deity on its currency. Therefore, the only god America *really* knows and honors is money.

Despite the actions of many individuals and many sections of the American society that indicate the true nature of our being, the impression made on many of our species outside these borders is one of colonial arrogance. This impression comes primarily from those who make up what is called the government.

There are over 285 million citizens that make up the nation-state that calls itself America. Of this number, only a fraction of the total citizen count make up what is called the 'government' at any given moment. The events of the last election should finally drive home the point that this is indeed NOT a representative government, but one that is controlled by a select group of individuals that belong to an exclusive gang, as it were.

Let's do a few numbers at this point:

• president*	1
• vice president*	1
• senators*	100
• representatives* (+/- 10)	450
• cabinet members* (+/- 3)	20
• military cabinet members* (+/- 1)	5
• subordinate cabinet posts# (civilian)	500
• subordinate cabinet posts# (military	250
• support staff for each primary position (all with *)	5,770
• support staff for each secondary position (all with #)	2,250
	9,347

These numbers will, no doubt, come under scrutiny and attack. However, my purpose is to indicate to the reader that out of the approximate 285 million citizens that make up what is called America at this point in time, only a handful are part of the 'government' as we know it. Even if another 10,000 or so souls were added to this list, it would still constitute a small gang within the American total population. If these numbers are too large, then it would indicate that an even smaller number of citizens make up the 'government.' This small cadre of people is supposed to represent us all.

Each citizen has his or her own reality of what America is and what it represents. Many of today's national makeup do not agree with the policies as determined by those at the top of this rather small group of people. Consequently, it is necessary for those of us who are not being heard to speak out in other fashions.

At this point in time, the same type of human being-white males, controls the vast majority of the wealth generated by this system. With their history of constant warfare and disdain for things non-white, it is vital that other voices begin to be heard. America has yet to find its true personality and identity. The identity of world leader is based on my white brother's illusion of military might. The previous great military system went broke and collapsed because its citizens refused to support it any longer.

Until the citizens change the direction and distribution of the wealth of this adolescent society, we will all continue to be distracted with the prevailing attitudes of this one member of our species. Recent events in Italy and New York have indicated that it is time to rethink how America uses its intellect and wealth.

We really need to talk.

And Then Some

That little something extra is what the world demands,
for the life you now have,
for the way you can run and the creations you do with your hands.

That little something extra is what the world does need,
to overcome the pall of profits and credits,
and to wipe out the oppressive cloud of greed.

That little something special is what the Earth awaits,
for the thoughts you have from the cradle on,
there's no rush and it's never too late.

That little something special is what our planet needs,
to change our programmed ethnics and
dispel the false doctrine of races and creeds.

That little something added is what the world will find
when fear is dispelled by the opened eye,
and the veils are removed from our mind.

That little something extra is what this play is about,
and much energy is spent to keep this fact down
and preventing us from finding out.

That little something other than what is required of you,
gives momentum to life, and promotes total health
and permits you to see what can be true.

Sylmar
1982

Ding, Dong—Doors Closing!!

Those of you who only know how to get around the planet in automobiles and other single-occupant vehicles will probably not appreciate this story or even understand the humor. In any event, this is a mass transit story.

We used to have lots and lots of trains dashing around all over the place in these-yet-to-be-United States. Most of those in our population who actually remember riding on the old systems are dwindling to some extent. Slowly but surely, however, individual cities and regions are recognizing the sheer stupidity of putting all our transportation eggs in one basket. Train systems are slowly re-appearing on the American landscape. In addition, the insanity associated with the oil guys, and all that entails, is finally beginning to hit many Americans in the head.

Ultimately, 9/11 was about oil and money.

So, this train story takes place in Baghdad by the Bay, up in Northern Cali.

It's the mid 80s.

The train system in question is called BART-stands for Bay Area Rapid Transit. It's classified as light rail. Overall, these guys run a pretty tight ship—upwards to 93% on-time rate. Not too shabby!! It's really amazing that the dumb thing got built at all, particularly in a state where the oil, car and concrete guys call most of the shots. It was started around

1972 and has continually grown, despite opposition from some of the strangest people and places. It was reported that when Fort Worth got their transit system built, it would be called FART.

As is the pattern across the entire planet, these trains systems are built underground in the financial districts of our cities and at ground level or slightly elevated away from the city centers. Downtown San Francisco has four underground stations and I was in the Montgomery Street Station where this story took place.

I was working in one of those high rise buildings crammed together in that seven-square mile city. As is the daily procedure 'en todo el mundo', when the quittin' bell sounds, people head for home. While the SF streets are jammed with autos and trucks, many who live in the East Bay take BART to go home. The locals take MUNI, the hometown transit system that serves San Francisco and the immediate areas. This system also has light-rail trains as well.

Of all the places I've traveled that have train systems, the folks in the Bay Area seem to be the most polite that you'd ever want to meet. That's not to say that other folks in other places are not polite also, but it was my observation that the Oakland and SF habit was to form orderly lines to wait for your train to arrive.

When this story unfolded, there were only four major lines to the system. Three served the East Bay and one served the West Bay. At the end of the work day, the trains ran approximately three minutes apart. Going toward the East Bay, they ran in alphabetical order. Concord, Fremont and Richmond were the ends of the three lines in the East Bay. After descending to the second level underground (the first level held the MUNI trains), passengers would queue up to wait for their trains. People would be holding brief cases, listening to personal radios, reading newspapers, etc. while waiting for their respective train. As a train would approach the station, the operator would—"toot! toot!" or some other combination of horn sounds, probably to wake up anyway who had dozed and was standing too close to the platform edge.

On this particular day, I'm standing about four people from the front of the left line. Usually, two lines would form at each place where a coach door would line up. As I had come down the escalator, I saw that a Richmond train, the one I wanted, was just pulling out. No matter, another one would be along in a few more minutes at this time of day. So I joined a line. There were light conversations here and there and the occasional rustle of newspapers as a train going in the opposite direction to Daly City would enter and leave the station.

It was then that the star of this story spoke up.

A well-dressed gentleman asked one of the standees how to get to the Oakland Airport. As I mentioned earlier, those Bay Area folk are helpful to a fault (actually most of our species are, when given half the chance). So before this guy knew it, several of us in those two lines had chimed in to give him the required data he sought. One woman mentioned that the Oakland Airport was on the Fremont line and he would have to get off at the Coliseum station and take a shuttle. She didn't know how much the shuttle was. I knew this fact, so I spoke up and told him that it would $1 to take the shuttle from the Coliseum station to the airport and they ran about every 12 minutes or so. As this conversation was going on, a Concord train pulled into the station, stopped, the doors opened and those who wanted that train filed in. "Boing" went the door closing signal and the doors closed. With the usual whine of those electric train motors and the attendant rush of wind, the 10-car train dashed away.

By this time, others had joined the lines but a few were still waiting on the either a Richmond or Fremont train. Our visitor's face was covered with this look of surprise. I took the chance to elaborate that the trains ran in alphabetical order and that the next train would probably be his, unless a second Concord train would come in. This was the case. Since a greater number of people lived on that line, a second train would sometimes follow the first one. The lines had gotten pretty long by now and most of them got on this second Concord train. When this train dashed off, our visitor's face grew even more astonished.

He asked about how late the system ran and a guy standing behind me promptly answered his question. Somewhere in all this conversation, someone had mentioned that his entire trip to the Oakland Airport wouldn't take more than 25-30 minutes or so.

It was then that he made the following statement:

"This is fantastic. So little time to the airport. It's just like science fiction."

That got everybody's attention. Several in the assembled lines asked, almost en masse:

"Where are you from"?

"Los Angeles", came his reply.

Changing Realities

There are approximately 290 million realities that make up the nation-state that calls itself by its various appellations-The States, America, USA, United States, Land of the Free, Columbia, Stateside, Home of the Brave, etc., etc., etc.

Each citizen has his or her own idea of what this adolescent entity was, is, or could be. It's with an emphasis on what America could be that I direct my attention.

As I perceive how the energies of the cosmos can be directed (consciously or un-consciously) and used by each individual, a small number of individuals has the present ability to influence the direction of this nation-state more so than most others.

The results of the 2000 presidential election should remind the reader of this fact.

Those who find themselves with great material wealth, as defined presently, would appear to have more of this "influence". An individual who finds himself to be in the position of "the leader" in any collection of realities would also appear to have more of this influence.

However, as our particular political system matures, more and more of us have come to realize that the elusive condition of equality is dispensed to some in greater proportion than to others—ergo, *some are more equal than others*—some have more power and influence than others.

How is this possible, you might ask?

Most of our species that are aware of the United States instinctively recognize the potential it represents. This recognition has nothing to do with economic status. However, there are far too many who believe they are the "directors" of this enterprise because they have attained a certain economic status or structural prominence. These individuals have arrived at this conclusion based on brief planetary historical precedent and selectively edited written narratives that support this same conclusion.

When Charles Darwin published the findings from his observations of the animal kingdom, his opinions were translated into various social settings throughout the human family. In the United States, the monetary system used became the guideline by which human endeavors were measured and a particular version of social Darwinism developed. Granted, other western nations adopted this social application of a biological theory, but the American version became the standard by which others were measured, at least in American eyes.

Unfortunately, a particular type of American myopia developed at the same time.

As our species continues to age and the increase in human numbers begins to affect the overall living situation of the entire planet, the various social systems that have been used up to this point in time are developing signs of operational stress.

We must now examine our present concepts of equality and how it is dispensed, as it were. This examination would, of necessity, include an analysis of the present American need to define human existence in terms of material acquisition.

You are nothing if you own nothing.

In other words, those with more are better and are more qualified to exist than those with less.

This line of thinking led some of us in America to experiment with selective sterilization of citizens who were deemed "unfit" by those who had given themselves the authority to pass judgment. Such experiments were carried out in the United States in the early part of the third decade of the last century. It was these particular experiments that gave the leaders of the doomed Third Reich their flawed ideas of genetic superiority.

> *The ancient concept of high and low birth*
> *is not the same. Under that system*
> *one did have the right to exist regardless.*

The vast majority of the human family who came to this continent during the colonial phase of the European tribes were, naturally, Europeans or whites. Having gone through centuries of needless religious wars and conflicts, many left that sad arena out of desperation and frustration. Life for the non-gentry class was appalling for most. By the time the second industrial revolution started, millions of European family members had come to these shores. Aided by ancient religious propaganda, all other human family members were considered subhuman and not included in the newly developing American dream. Consequently, to most Anglos, America was theirs and theirs alone. Others family members who lived here were just part of the scenery.

> *You can cook my food, cut my lawn,*
> *clean my home, drive my car,*
> *watch after my kids,*
> *but don't have an opinion.*

After the two white tribal wars of the 20th century, other family members began to question their exclusion from "the system". Legal battles to end forced separation of the races were fought and won, putting to the test the high-sounding words written in the document that is supposedly the philosophical foundation of the present system.

There is still, however, a small but determined core of white males who want to perpetuate the idea that America is for them and them alone. Unfortunately for them, as Carlos Fuentes said, "We are all becoming each other."

As more and more members of the human family migrate to these shores, the complexion and apparent reality of this present nation-state is undergoing inevitable change. No one notices this more than the aforementioned white males. The media, an industry controlled primarily by this one type of our species, is constantly noting the fact that the face of the nation is changing and this or that group is growing in numbers. My white brother went about the planet bragging about his "way of life". To his surprise and utter consternation, these other guys have shown up.

DUH!!!

We're all living on the same planet. Consequently, we all have the right to live where we choose, artificial borders notwithstanding. The hard realities of the life pattern of our species are one of interchange, trade and intermingling. This re-joining of the species, as it were, would have happened anyway had those clans of Europe not been forced into darkness and arrogant ignorance by the church. The style of this re-joining would not have been as chaotic.

In our present era, our species is undergoing a revision of facts as the attitudes and thinking patterns of the colonial ethic are slowly being replaced by more balanced points of view.

The realities are changing.

Stay tuned.

Dominu, Gobbi Gobbinus, Domino

As mentioned elsewhere in this collection of essays, modern civilization, as we have come to know it, is basically a male concept. The design, working structure, operation and overall direction or mis-direction, is all from the male perspective. To achieve this end, the religious dogma used in what is called Western Civilization eliminated the presence of the female in that dogma. Of the three primary religious sects of the west, Judaism is the least offensive to the female of the species. However, it is from the creation myth of this particular religion that the other two major Western religions derive their concepts and attitudes about the female of our species.

Western civilizations prior to the so-called Christian era are all located in the (B.C.) B.C.E. date-time space. This arbitrary division of the time line, in the western sense, is just that, arbitrary and self-serving.

Western tribes from the European continent and their subsequent off-spring consider themselves the most advanced of the species at this stage of the planetary game. The ancient cultures, of which Kemet (Egypt) is the most prominent, were not as heavily stacked against the female as are the later systems. In addition, their cultural focus was entirely different that those cultures of our time.

A cursory glance at past and present planetary human societies, in general, reveals a particular structural pattern—mainly different classes of species members who dispense laws and/or directives and control the monetary system. Most members of any given society are not part of this law-dispensing or money class. These citizens must look to these leader individuals for answers and guidance in life matters that go beyond the thoughts and immediate capabilities of those **not** part of this law-dispensing or money holding class. For a lack of a better word, we shall call these individuals priests or priest classes.

In the ancient world of Kemet, the priest class controlled the knowledge that became known to us in our time as the Mysteries. It was some of this knowledge that was briefly mentioned in the Bible when Moses (a name taken from the latter part of a pharaoh's name) did battle with the priests of the particular pharaoh on the throne when the exodus took place.

> *Those popular walking sticks and the*
> *symbol of priestly office became serpents.*
> *It was a battle of symbols and magical power.*
> *Moses had been to Delpi.*

Since the story of this exodus was told by those who left Kemet, we've only been presented with just one side of the events in question and the outcome of this little drama. Not all the members of that tribe left Kemet.

> *As it is in all human events, there are always*
> *two sides to every story, sometimes more.*

We've never heard from the ones from this tribe who stayed in Kemet.

I wonder why.

As the veil of darkness was lifted from the minds of the tribes of Europe, trade increased and so did the amount of money coming into their various homelands. The first group to gain prominence in the Italian city-states were the merchants. Soon after them came the law-yers, followed shortly by the moneychangers or bankers. Those who tallied or kept track of money came into being almost as quickly.

In the purely American culture, there are presently four priest classes. Their common street names are bankers, lawyers, doctors and bean counters. Their formal names are financiers, attorneys, physicians and accountants. They all have historical connection to the old guilds systems that existed in early Europe and other older societies across the planet. In the guild system, young males were taught the trade or craft of their fathers, who in turn had been taught this particular knowledge by their fathers, etc., etc., etc.

In the world of today, those who aspire to benefit from the social and financial status attainable in these priesthoods do so by acquiring various educational degrees. By attending institutions of higher learning, they can obtain the necessary knowledge required by a particular priesthood. When degrees are conferred, the individual becomes an acolyte in his or her chosen profession. As expected, females are generally not allowed to progress too far in this male-dominated architecture; however, even that is beginning to change in these times of great upheaval.

Those in the medical guild spend the longest amount of time and money in preparation for "service" in this area. Little wonder that 45% of our present citizenry cannot afford health care in any form. Most medical types are in debt up to their ears when they start their careers as medical priests. Most gravitate to the largest urban centers to recoup their losses. As a result of this concentration on money, many rural areas have gone without medical representation for some time. An interesting situation has developed concurrently—physicians who were trained in other nations are now serving many rural areas. Most American types want to be rich and famous, as it were, and go where the money is. We are still robbing other lands of their talent. First it was slavery for their physical strength and now this appalling set of circumstances of stealing their best minds.

Those in the legal guild operate in a similar fashion. Just pick up the yellow page directory of any major metropolitan center and look at the number of attorneys listed. One directory I noticed recently had even changed the color of the pages that listed the attorneys. That way they can be found easily.

Most citizens of present-day America are aware of what an accountant is—something to do with money management, or mis-management, as we have all learned recently. This is youngest of the priest classes to arise in Western society. In fact, most decisions made today in both the political and non-political areas of our system are made with accounting principles in mind, or at the foundation of the approach.

> *John D. Rockerfeller was a bookkeeper.*
> *The oil guys were good at finding oil*
> *but couldn't manage their money.*
> *He could, did so, and took his cut.*
> *He was also a Baptist.*

As stated earlier, all human systems have had priest classes of one form or another.

The Jesuit priests were sent by the Catholic Church to learn the political and financial setup of the new societies over which it sought to gain control. It took the church about 200 years to turn these guys off. They were not successful in some instances, however. The Japanese, much to their credit, soon saw them for what they were and evicted them from their land. All of us were not deceived.

It's about land and mineral wealth.
Spirituality and peace never had anything to do with it.

In the popular religious media of today, the vast amount of discourse concerns itself with the right to live "well" as promised by the god of the American version of the creator as described in that bible. Since this particular book has been greatly altered and various sects are producing their own versions, it is little wonder to discover all the various interpretations of the "word". Depending upon the outlook of the speaker, primarily males, one can get a veritable smorgasbord of the "word". There are still those versions that contend that the white tribes are the true bringers of the word and all others are damned. Some have even built universities to perpetuate this concept.

The second largest single land-owning entity in the present United States is the Catholic Church. The first, of course, is the federal government. Check out the location of the buildings belonging to the various "main-stream" denominations throughout the land. Prime locations usually have churches or synagogues on them.

It's those males and their way of thinking again.

Presently, there are considerable numbers joining hands to eliminate the separation of church and state that is written into the constitution. First one must ask why the founding fathers (no mothers, we notice) saw fit to put such language in that bold and forwarding-looking document.

The last time we had the church and state together as a government, we got a little episode in human history called The Inquisition. The founding fathers were aware of this and sought to prevent the same thing from happening in this land. Those in America who want to return to that condition are totally unaware of the damage done to certain members of our species and the world in general when that system was allowed to develop. Some of my white brothers are so ignorant about a lot of things, especially their own tribal past. Most don't remember or know of the carnage caused to their own tribes by religion.

In our time, the Catholic Church, as represented by the present CEO (Pope John), finally admitted that they were wrong about a certain Italian teacher and his views about our place in the cosmos. He was telling folk that we were not at the center of the universe and that we moved around the sun, not the other way around as the church had been telling everyone. It was the Inquisition that gave them the power to put that man under house arrest to shut him up.

However, some of his students and followers were not so fortunate. Those guys were burned at the stake in various places, especially in Spain.

> *It only took them 400 years to*
> *admit their mistake.*
> *About fuckin' time.*

More recently, this prelate made a member of the Aztec tribe a saint. He asked that we [mainly first-world people (white folk)] treat these humans better from now on. I had it pointed out to me that such statements and actions are of no value. This man is near death and wants to clear his conscience. Such actions on his part would have produced a greater impact if he had said and done these things at a much younger age, say when he first became pope.

Some of the religious idiots we find on the American national scene today want to return to those days where the church makes the laws. That's all they have in their little battered brains. Most of them, predictably, are white males. Better keep your eyes on these guys-they're scary!

As someone once said, those who do not learn from the past are doomed to repeat it.

Veneers

The definition of the word veneer as written by Merriam Webster is as follows:

a layer of wood of superior value or excellent grain to be glued to an inferior wood

This is the first definition. The third definition, as used within our language, is:

a superficial or deceptively attractive appearance, display, or effect: facade

With the exception of the physical and non-physical characteristics passed along in our genetic code sequences, all humans are an amalgam of various types of veneers—coverings and layers added to the personality after the individual is born. Many of the veneers of individuals and collections of individuals are deceptively attractive.

As the individual proceeds along his or her particular time line, forces outside the physical and non-physical sphere of that person place layers of attitudes and beliefs on them as the individual adds more and more days to his time line and existence.

Primary sources for most of our veneers come from the various family units that humans form. The core values of an individual get their start here. If no recognizable family unit is present during the first 3-4 years of life, that individual absorbs the values of the immediate world in which he finds himself. The so-called "latch key kids" are an example of what can happen to an individual when there is no consistent guidance as growth occurs. Secondary sources for human veneers were generally found in the community at large, reinforced and supported by customs and traditions that existed in all human cultures, no matter their origin. Places of worship, schools, various social organizations were an additional source and reinforcement of the values started at the primary source.

However, after the second great white tribal war, the American society became splintered. The community forces that filled in the blanks when family units experienced death, illness, loss of fortune or other negative forces were replaced with nothing. Individual family units, no matter their individual structure, eventually were left to fend for themselves and did not have the community support that existed prior to the advent of the automobile.

As our cities became larger and larger and the time required to go back and forth from point A to point B became longer, the identity of the individual has become fused with the mode of transportation chosen to do all this traveling. In today's world a person is known by what type of vehicle he or she drives. Many individuals will never buy a home but most certainly will purchase many cars before they die. The automobile has become a mechanical veneer. Owning one gives status, or the illusion of status, to the owner. The more money a person acquires, the larger or more expensive the automobile a person generally buys. There are exceptions, of course, to this general rule of thumb and such individuals are termed "eccentric", particularly if that individual has great wealth–a veneer attached by others.

> *Those without wealth make do*
> *with what they can get.*
> *It's the veneer of poverty.*

Human beings are all born blank—with a clean slate, so to speak. The family unit and the culture in which that family unit is located become the foundation upon which the individual begins to accumulate the veneers that eventually make up the person we meet on the street.

The veneers of nationalism and religious identity are probably the most easy to recognize. Other veneers are more subtle but upon close inspection can be seen as something that has been added to the individual after their appearance on the planet.

There are no genetic codes for national identity, religious identity or cultural identity, despite the protestations of so-called experts. All of these human factors are added after the fact and are, by definition, veneers.

> *If a veneer is something that is added after birth,*
> *it follows that it is also something that can be removed.*

Eye color (at least the original one) cannot be changed, nor can the original color of the skin or hair. Height and weight are factors determined by genetic code sequences and may, in the future, be manipulated for one reason or another. However, at this point in time, these non-veneer human factors are pretty static.

Anything else making up the personality of any human is a veneer, plain and simple. The primary driving force for the formation of the multitude of organizations that people form is to be able to recognize a veneer and to associate with those with similar veneer patterns. As stated elsewhere in these essays, all human organizations are ways to associate oneself with those like one's self. Being with others whose veneers are different can sometimes be unsettling and, in many cases, frightening.

This fear of "veneer difference" is the primary foundation for warfare. The enemy has to be created, his veneer difference pointed out in order to organize action against this threat to the security of the group who doesn't want to or is incapable of accepting veneer difference.

In the last of the tribal wars of Europe, the veneer differences of the Slavic foreign workers were used to get the German citizens to ban these workers from their country. Prior to this action, many old people and babies that were considered "not perfect" (incorrect veneers) were done away with because they were seen as a drain on the economy. As the power of the military machine grew, those with other different veneers eventually became the targets of that same machine. By the end of this second tribal war, we all had learned what madness had taken place because of veneer difference.

When the foundation of a society is based solely on the attainment of material wealth or acquired veneers, it becomes rather easy to dismiss those who do not fit the "norm" of the larger group or who do not have the correct 'veneer'.

> *Western religions, as we have come to understand them,*
> *teach intolerance toward anything that is different.*
> *An early term of sociology is group think.*
> *"You don't have the correct religious veneer."*

The adolescent nation-state called America has seen fit to try to isolate a neighboring nation-state called Cuba because the latter chose a different path in the management of their society. The colonial conceited arrogance of the American system permits it to assume that its point of view is the correct one for itself and everyone else on the planet. Much misery has been heaped upon the small island nation. This tiny nation-state simply chose a different political veneer. At the beginning of this present millennium, lively discussions are being carried on about the wisdom of continuing these negative actions against this part of the human family. The futility and lack of reasoning can be seen and the actions taken by the United States are undergoing a welcome change.

Many of those with power and vast wealth are the most frightened of changes or damage to their veneers and will resort to any means necessary, including political assassinations, to insure the continuity of their acquired veneers.

Take a look around in your particular region of the planet and see if you can recognize these coverings.

Just Who Do You Think You Are,—Anyway? No, Anyhow, His Cousin.

We Americans are an adolescent collection of humans that calls itself a nation. On our planet, there are many other collections of humans living here as well, many of them much older than the one I find myself living in. In one sense, the land called US is a young teenager, say around 15½ or so. Those collections called New Zealand and Australia are almost a set of twins, or at least very close siblings. They're about nine or ten years old now. On the other hand, as a matter of contrast, Israel is a noisy two-year-old that's been spoiled by its big brother, the land of US. A teenager does not have the experience to be a disciplinarian, so this desert brat is out of control.

Those human collections that carried out the dubious practice of colonizing the planet are all in their 80s now. They learned the hard way that colonizing was not the thing to do. The colonizing effect interrupted the natural growth of many family collections and most of them are just now sorting all this inflicted mess out. Most of these collections damaged by colonization are re-discovering their original personalities and their ages as well.

Many of the societies that developed on the African continent have even had to rename themselves in addition to finding their own pasts. This is a time-consuming process and will not be done overnight. Applying one of Sir Isaac's laws to these processes would indicate that an equal amount of time is needed to reverse the effects of colonization. Since these collections did not count time in the manner familiar to westerners, we may never know fully how old these various collections are.

One of the most ancient collections appeared on the African continent. When the Greeks went to Kemet, it was ancient to them at that time. We have recent evidence that human activity in this collection may reach back as far as 10K or so years.

Those collections in the Indian sub-continent and in China and other parts of what is called Asia are much older than most of the collections in the west.

Any collection that underwent a personality shift, in essence, has died. The collection known as Rome had its personality shifted by the church. Likewise, during the time of the original collection that the world knows as Rome, the Judeans, now known as Israelis, had their collective activity terminated. Consequently, these present personalities are new ones to the human family. Many others from the time of the original Romans and Judeans are no longer with us.

Other human collections are considerably older that the ones I've mentioned so far. My teenage nation was misguided enough to attack and damage one of the oldest human collections and personalities recently. Now known as Iraq, Mesopotamia is one of the oldest collections of humans with an equally ancient personality. Greece, Macedonia and Turkey are in the neighborhood of this age group. Despite the effects of this religious era, most of these very old collections have maintained their original personalities.

We are just now recognizing that the societies that lived on this side of the planet before the colonizers arrived are from a part of the human collective past that is far older than previously thought. As mentioned elsewhere in these essays, the genetic, planetary and human memories of those humans called aborigines may be older than any other part of the human family.

Recent translations of the Mayan and Aztec glyphs indicate a different planetary and cosmic attitude than the one taught in this land. They speak of a connection between the planet and the spiritual growth of our species. Personally, I have learned more about the non-physical part of our existence from the writings and philosophy of the mis-named American Indian than I have from anything from the Judeo-Christian camp. These latter guys have their focus on this up-coming war of theirs and that's tired and predictable.

I, for one, find this other part of the human history more credible than what I hear from the noisy religious zealots of this country. If you're tired of the predictable nature of the "forecasts of doom", go check out this part of the human planetary history for yourself.

Sorry, but We Have to Leave.

We humans have been living in this planet for untold thousands of years. However, our collective memories and records of our comings and goings have been altered by the actions of the planet itself. When she goes through the phases of her own life cycle, the results of our collective actions, whatever they may or might have been, are, in most cases, wiped out or severely damaged. Any structure built by us is fair game when it comes time to recycle a continent.

On this side of the planet, the legend of Atlantis persists to this day, despite the ramblings of the so-called experts. Those triangle things, the one off the coast of Florida and the one over in the Philippines are reminders that a lot has been going on that we really don't understand. There are parts of our system, namely the war guys, who have been keeping track on all this stuff but don't want to talk to anyone about because of their fears. It must be unsettling to tell everyone that you're on top of everything, in control and all that dribble, only to be constantly reminded that you're not. It's part of that male denial thing I mentioned elsewhere. Just lie about it. Classify it secret and the public will ignore what's been happening.

Structures such as all those mono-or megaliths strewn throughout the British Isles, all the planetary structures done in stone without the benefit of 'modern technology' and the mathematics involved to construct these items are relentless reminders that we're missing great blocks of our collective history as a species on this planet.

We haven't given up on learning how those guys in Kemet and Central American built those pyramids. However, the usual human events that occupy our attention are really designed to keep most of us distracted. We can't have too many embarrassing questions put before those who are supposed to be in charge, now can we?

In addition, the fact that our planet seems to have been visited by other sentient beings is another topic that's couched in mystery and deception. From my standpoint, that conceited arrogance of my white brother I mentioned elsewhere keeps a lot of us from seriously talking about such possibilities. While the usual groups of white boys jockey for political and financial one-upsmanship, others on our darling planet have come to realize that there are many more important and vital topics that we all should be pondering.

For me, it appears that the physical records of our species have been wiped out whenever the planet flips and settles back into her routine afterwards. Fables and fragments of information about human events prior to and after these planetary changes are all that we have left. Coupled with the fact that certain groups have taken it upon themselves to actually burn and destroy records of past ancient human societies only adds insult to injury. Talk about dark ages. We're in one right now.

Consequently, now that we've developed the mechanical ability to actually leave the planet, build space stations that become satellites to our home and develop a system of dependable travel to and from such structures, the possibility of maintaining species continuity is now within our reach.

With so many fragments of our collective past scattered all over the place and the predominance of things that are supposed to be important clogging the airwaves, it's little wonder that the air battles and space wars mentioned in the Gita are never talked about. Then there's Ezekial and his observations that are part of the book called the Bible. Just what did this man see?

To call something anecdotal is how those who are frightened the most dismiss the individual human's observations. I guess there's a little bit of the doubting Thomas in each of us.

The technology of today that we accept as fact (electronic media, jets, shuttles, etc.) would be a miracle to someone from the 16th century, if not downright frightening. Individuals such as Leonardo, Nicolas or Benjamin could grasp this new knowledge, but most would run in fear and panic.

I have used the term continuity to indicate that a continuous thread of total human activity on our planet is available to us for the first time in our brief recorded history. This opportunity has come about because we now have the ability to live off the planet in *relative* stability.

Stability, security and other such terms have no meaning in the real world. When all of us are carrying out our individual and collective dreams on a planet that is rotating at it's present rate and also swimming in the vastness of space, the idea of something being "stable" is another one of those false concepts from that conceited and arrogant mind I have mentioned earlier.

Our planet is slowly and inexorably working her way up to rearranging the furniture a bit and we should be using this remaining time before that event to collect, store and record all human knowledge off-world. We should also start moving as many of us off-world as well. It's nice that the military types have done their part, but from the standpoint of the entire family, the ever-inventive citizen is better at such endeavors than is the reactive military mind.

Our home planet is alive and has a life of her own. What we think is important really isn't. She is not interested in our affairs and continues on her own in spite of us. Rantings and ravings from various groups who claim to have the answers are a waste of media time and printer's ink.

For you white folks, legends from an ancient part of my tribe tell us that life on this planet came from elsewhere, near a binary star system with a white dwarf companion. At the outset of these essays, I said that we really don't know if we are from here, this planet. After the next earthquake, think on these thoughts from a black member of the species.

As far as I'm concerned, it's really time for us to leave.

Fun at His Expense

◆

(Courtesy of the Web)

All babies start out with the same number of raw cells, which over nine months, develop into a complete female baby. The problem occurs when cells are instructed by the stunted Y chromosome to make a male baby instead. Because there are only so many cells to go around, the cells necessary to develop a male's reproductive organs have to come from cells already assigned elsewhere in the female.

Recent tests have shown that these cells are removed from the communications center of the brain, which then migrate to a lower part of the body and develop into male sexual organs. If you visualize a normal brain to be similar to a full deck of cards, this means that males are born a few cards short, so to speak, and some of these cards are in their shorts.

This difference between the male and female brain manifests itself in various ways. Little girls will tend to play things like house or learn to read. Little boys, however, will tend to do things like placing a bucket over their heads and running into walls. This basic cognitive difference continues to grow until puberty, when the hormones kick into action and the trouble really begins.

After puberty, not only the size of the male and female brains differ, but the center of thought also differs. Women think with their heads. Male thoughts often originate lower in their bodies where their ex-brain cells reside.

Of course, the size of this problem varies from male to male. In some men only a small number of brain cells migrate and they are left with nearly full mental capacity but they tend to be rather dull, sexually speaking. Such men are known in medical terms as "Engineers." Other men suffer larger brain cell relocation. These men are medically referred to as "Fighter Pilots." A small number of men suffer massive brain cell migration to their groins. These men are usually referred to as..."Mr. President or Mr. Congressman".

◆   ◆   ◆

We are informed by the State of Alaska Wildlife Commission that *all* reindeer produce antlers annually. The males, however, loose their antlers toward the end of November and grow them again in the spring. On the other hand, the females retain theirs through winter and loose them just prior to giving birth to the new fawns in the spring.

We should have known.

Only a bunch of females, pregnant no less, could drag a fat guy in a red suit around in the snow without getting lost.

0-595-26165-5

www.ingramcontent.com/pod-product-compliance
Lightning Source LLC
Chambersburg PA
CBHW020915290526
45784CB00002BA/569